TOO CLOSE TO HOME: THE SAMANTHA ZALDIVAR CASE

STEPHEN C. TARBELL with L. L. WALLACE

LLW Enterprises LLC

Cover designs and photo by Jesaro Photography

L.L. Wallace Photo by Hannah Whaley Photography

Copyright © 2017

Stephen C. Tarbell and Laurinda L. Wallace

All rights reserved.

For information contact: LLW Enterprises LLC ● PO Box 415 ● Hereford, AZ 85615.

ISBN-13:978-1546626473

ISBN-10:1546626476

FOREWORD

When Steve Tarbell approached me a couple of years ago about writing a book with him, it took me by surprise, but my curiosity was piqued. The memoir he had in mind was about one of the most notorious cases in Wyoming County, where I lived most of my life. It was one that touched every family in the Letchworth Central School District—the same school district which my daughters attended. I daresay it affected every community in Wyoming County and throughout New York State.

As a lifelong resident of Wyoming County until 2003 and a Letchworth grad myself, I believe the story of law enforcement's efforts in bringing a measure of justice to an innocent young girl needs to be told. It's also an account of the extraordinary community response to search for seven-year-old Samantha Zaldivar.

This book is a behind-the-scenes look at the anatomy of a criminal investigation—the processes, long hours, attention to detail, and commitment to solve a case. It is the story of men and women who did their absolute best in their work as police officers, forming a multi-agency team that was able to operate effectively to catch a murderer.

Law enforcement officers are under more pressure than ever, and their mission to protect and serve us has become exponentially more dangerous. Sadly, we hear about many officers losing their lives in the line of duty all too often. The job isn't easy—not for officers or their families. Police work comes first: before spouses, kids, and a social life. It's a life of sacrifice as it is for our military and other first responders. We need reminders that police officers are dads, moms, brothers, sisters, sons, and daughters, just like us. They see people at their worst and at their most vulnerable. Without regard for their own personal safety, they are on the front lines every day, working to keep us safe in a dangerous world.

It has been a pleasure and an honor to work with Steve on this project. I hope readers will gain a better understanding of the dedication law enforcement have for their work and the diligence of those who labor for justice in our courts.

Laurinda L. Wallace
June 2017

ACKNOWLEDGMENTS

We gratefully acknowledge the cooperation and support of the Wyoming County Sheriff's Department (WCSO); Sheriff Gregory J. Rudolph; former Sheriff Farris Heimann; Undersheriff David Linder; the Wyoming County District Attorney's Office; Donald G. O'Geen, District Attorney; Wyoming County Attorney James Wujcik; and Wyoming County Records Manager Gail Royce. Without their help, this book would not have been possible.

Special thanks to: Wyoming County Sheriff Allen Capwell (retired); WCSO Sergeant Investigator Gary Eck (retired); WCSO Investigator Dennis Spink (retired); Timothy Crino (former FBI Evidence Response Team Leader); Special NYS Investigator Harold Frank (retired); Hon. Mark H. Dadd, Wyoming County Judge (retired); Wyoming County District Attorney Gerald L. Stout (retired); Special NYS Prosecutor Diane LaVallee; Wyoming County Public Defender Norman Effman; Wyoming County Coroner Michael Smith; David DiMatteo (former Wyoming County ADA); and Town of Wethersfield Historian Lisa Johnson. Each gave generously of their time and expertise.

Note: Rachel Stra declined our request for an interview.

This book is based upon police reports, photographs, court documents, media accounts, recollections of Stephen C. Tarbell, and interviews with retired law enforcement officers, attorneys, and others with personal knowledge of the Samantha Zaldivar case. Every attempt at accuracy has been made in relating the story; however, we recognize that memories are sometimes imperfect, and even our best efforts at accuracy will fall short. Some names have been changed to protect the individual's privacy and are indicated with *.

In Memoriam

Over the span of my career with the Wyoming County Sheriff's Office, I spent a lot of time with these three coworkers who worked tirelessly on this case. My thoughts and prayers go out to these three and their families. *S. C. T.*

Undersheriff Ronald B. Ely

1946-2012

Investigator David J. Davis

1942-2014

Investigator Paul R. Donnelly

1959-2015

1997

Wyoming County Sheriff's Department

Road Patrol Roster

Sheriff Allen Capwell

Undersheriff Ronald Ely

Captain John Copeland

Sergeant Investigator Gary Eck

Sergeant Kevin Gehman

Sergeant Michael Quinn

Sergeant David Linder

Sergeant Edward Till

Investigator David Davis

Investigator Larry May

Investigator Dennis Spink

Investigator Paul Donnelly

T/Sergeant Stephen Tarbell

Deputy Robert McElver

Deputy Garry Ingles

Deputy Daniel Hummel

Deputy Susan Omans

Deputy David Beardsley

T/Sergeant Farris Heimann

Deputy Ivan Carrasquillo

Deputy Joseph Mlyniec

Deputy Aaron Anderson

Deputy Daniel Perl

Deputy Jason Mayer

Deputy Lance Hanes

Deputy Matthew Felix

Deputy Steven Miller

Deputy Steven Stenson

CHAPTER 1

Wednesday, February 26, 1997

Life was about to take a drastic turn for me when I responded to a call about a missing girl on February 26, 1997. The case would consume me and test my skills as a law enforcement officer. For the next year-and-a-half, there would be inordinately long hours, frustrating dead-ends, and bizarre twists. The case would be front-page news in the local papers and even become a national news story during the course of the investigation. It would challenge the mettle and the resolve of the Wyoming County Sheriff's Office, the Wyoming County District Attorney, and all those who helped investigate to find the truth.

The Wyoming County Sheriff's Office in Warsaw, New York received the call at 4:31 PM. Seven-year-old Samantha Zaldivar was missing. According to her mother's boyfriend, Angel Colon, she hadn't gotten off the bus at the usual time of 3:15 to 3:30 PM. He'd been looking for her throughout the neighborhood without any success.

Dispatchers Sandy Tiede and Fred Ingles contacted Deputy Steven Miller, who within minutes returned the call to the residence to glean more information from Colon. After receiving a description of the first grader, who attended Donald F. Lockwood Elementary School in the Letchworth School District, Deputy Miller contacted Sergeant David Linder. The pair responded to the call, which had originated from the Hermitage Meadows Trailer Park in the tiny rural hamlet of Hermitage.

The dispatchers sent out a missing person notification to nine other county units within the sheriff's department along with a NYS Parks unit that also received the message. The county's law enforcement community flew into action to find Samantha. The first hours of finding a missing child are crucial.

Patches of melting snow bordered the circular driveway to the mobile home park near the fast-running Smith Creek. The stream fed into the larger East Koy Creek, and its dark, cold waters would swiftly carry a small child downstream. Winter seemed to be easing its grip on the countryside in late February, but below-freezing night temperatures were especially dangerous for a lost child who might be hurt or trapped in some way outdoors.

Sergeant Linder and Deputy Miller, the first on the scene, arrived a few minutes after 5:00 PM as twilight was settling into the bleak winter landscape. Walking through mud and traces of dirty snow, they knocked on the door of the trailer on Lot 36-G to interview Rachel Stra, Samantha's mother, and Angel Colon. Neighbors were at windows, watching the surreal drama play out before them. Children didn't disappear in Wyoming County. This was a safe place to raise your family. People knew one another and watched out for each other. But no one remembered seeing Samantha get off the school bus that afternoon. Angel Colon had called or knocked on their doors asking if they'd seen the pretty little girl with dark brown hair and eyes, who had such a bright smile. They hadn't seen her.

Linder and Miller began questioning Samantha's mother, Rachel Stra, who came out to the driveway to meet them. They were trying to quickly piece together the details of Tuesday evening and Wednesday. Angel Colon seemed reluctant to speak with them and left a few minutes later to pick up his and Rachel's two daughters from The Learning Center, a daycare center in Perry, NY, while the officers met with Rachel. Sitting at the kitchen table, twenty-six-year-old Rachel began recounting the details for the sergeant and deputy. She hadn't seen Samantha off to school that day. The mother of three with dark-brown hair and eyes explained she'd returned home early from her evening college class and because of illness had slept in that morning.

When the alarm woke her at 7:30 AM, Angel walked into the bedroom to tell her that Samantha had left for the bus minutes earlier. He'd gotten the first grader ready on Wednesday morning. Giving two photos of her daughter to the men, she related that after calling the school principal earlier, they'd discovered Samantha hadn't attended school that day. It appeared that Samantha hadn't made it to the bus. Someone could have taken her between 7:15 and 7:20 that morning. Or maybe she'd wandered away for some reason. The clock was ticking on locating Samantha. Over ten hours had passed. With darkness setting in, any search efforts would be difficult at best.

The Wyoming County Sheriff's Office serves and protects a rural county made up of farmland, small villages, and hamlets. Deputies cover an area of 596 square miles and serve a population of a little more than 40,000 residents. There were twenty-eight members of the Wyoming County Sheriff's Office at the time, which included the sheriff, undersheriff, a captain, sergeant investigator, four investigators, two technical sergeants, four sergeants, and fourteen deputies. Almost 7,000 complaints were logged in over the year in 1997. Resources were already stretched to the breaking point because of the enormous caseload. There were ongoing investigations into fatal fires, fatal motor vehicle accidents, a home invasion, rapes, burglaries, bodies found, larcenies, fraud, DWIs, and drug investigations. These didn't include the day-to-day normal calls for domestic matters and neighborhood complaints.

The urgency of finding Samantha quickly was foremost in the sheriff's mind. Without a K-9 search-and-rescue team (SAR), Sheriff Allen Capwell contacted nearby counties for assistance. Cattaraugus and Livingston counties responded immediately, sending K-9 officers and their dogs to the trailer park.

Wyoming County Deputy Miller began knocking on neighbors' doors while Sergeant Linder and Investigator Dennis Spink, who'd arrived to help, spoke with Angel Colon. He'd just returned with their daughters, three-year-old Angela and two-year-old Cassandra. Law enforcement radios crackled with news of more help on the way. Local fire departments had volunteers to join the K-9 searchers.

Linder met Colon as he entered the trailer with Angela and Cassandra, who ran to greet their mother. Angel walked past the sergeant and sat on the couch. He turned on the television while the sergeant asked about the time Samantha had gone out the door and what she was wearing. Colon was sure he'd sent her to the bus between 7:18-7:20. He was also sure she was wearing blue shorts, a blue shirt with red stripes, and a purple jacket. He thought she was about sixty-six pounds and four feet tall. The flashing lights of the cruisers shot eerie shadows through the quiet residential area as more officers drove in to assist in the search. Most of the neighbors had been visited by a deputy, asking about the last time they'd seen Samantha.

Sheriff Allen Capwell and Wyoming County Fire Coordinator Jack Fisher began setting up a command post at Rowe's General Store, located at the corner of Wethersfield Road and Route 78. Owner Elaine Rowe was glad to help in any way she could. This mainstay business in Hermitage provided a central location to coordinate the search. It was also only a few hundred yards from the trailer park, and the search would concentrate on that area. The store owner knew little Samantha, who often came to the store.

The water levels of East Koy Creek were rising rapidly due to melting snow runoff in this popular trout-fishing stream. Capwell and Fisher quickly handed out assignments to firemen and rescue personnel. The closest communities of Bliss, Gainesville, and Silver Springs responded to the sheriff's call for help in the search. New York State Police also came to the scene to lend a hand with the deputies and more than seventy-five volunteers. The men walked the soggy fields in the cold rain toward East Koy Creek, eyes straining to catch any sign of Samantha—a glimpse of a purple jacket or the child's backpack. They knew time was of the essence.

Once Deputy Morsch of the Livingston County Sheriff's Office arrived with his tracking dog, one of Samantha's shoes was given to the dog to identify her scent. The same process continued with the arrival of Deputy Krieger from Cattaraugus County and his dog. The teams began working the trailer park area, searching for any trace of the little girl. The Livingston County deputy and his K-9 partner Magnum found a strong scent near the trailer and driveway. They carefully covered the yard around the trailer and nearby sheds, attempting to pick up any trace of the girl. Then the pair methodically circled out farther in the mobile home park, and the dog didn't alert. The normal route that Samantha would have taken to catch the school bus didn't yield any results that would help identify where the little girl had gone. The deputy concluded that it was possible Samantha had left by vehicle from the trailer's driveway. Little did we know that months later this would prove to be correct.

The Cattaraugus SAR dog alerted to a scent route, which led out of the mobile home park. The dog, eager to follow the trail, strained at the leash and led Deputy Krieger down Wethersfield Road, toward Rowe's General Store. The dog stopped at the phone booth outside the store. The scent trail ended abruptly. Krieger determined that Samantha may have made it as far as the store and then someone picked her up.

With little else to go on, the search continued well into the night. Undersheriff Ron Ely and investigators arrived at Stra's trailer as more volunteers gathered at the command post down the road.

Sheriff Capwell called me to the scene at 7:42 PM to begin the process of evidence collection. The interviews with Colon and Stra had raised more questions. We needed answers to locate this little girl. There had to be a magic piece of information that would emerge so we would have a happy ending. I wanted to believe we would find her safe and sound. As the father of a ten-year-old son and thirteen-year-old daughter at the time, I couldn't begin to imagine what the family was experiencing. How would I react if one of my children disappeared? A string of questions buzzed in my head. Could someone have abducted her from the driveway on her way to the bus? Had she decided to skip school? Was she visiting a neighbor or friend? Where was Samantha Zaldivar?

CHAPTER 2

Wednesday, February 26, 1997

When Investigator Dennis Spink and Undersheriff Ron Ely joined the officers at the scene around 5:45 PM, Sergeant Linder immediately briefed them about the situation. Dennis recalled that when he pulled into the trailer court that night, he was overwhelmed with a strong sense that the incident would turn into a long investigation. That gut instinct would prove to be right.

Samantha was the biological child of Rachel Stra and Noel Zaldivar, who lived in Miami, Florida. The two other children in the household with Rachel and Angel were Angela and Cassandra, both said to be the biological offspring of Rachel and her fiancé, Angel Colon.

Once Spink entered the home, he asked Colon if he would speak to him privately outside. Colon consented and followed the investigator out to Spink's county vehicle.

Colon shared background information about moving the family of five to New York from Florida the previous summer. He'd had trouble keeping a job and was currently laid off from Champion Products in Perry. Colon gave details of the day before and the current day to the investigator. He'd helped Samantha with her homework and had given the three girls a bath together. After putting Samantha to bed around 9:00 PM, he'd watched television with his two daughters. Rachel had returned home from her college class around 9:30 PM. He'd stayed up late to watch a movie and had fallen asleep on the couch after the girls and Rachel had gone to bed.

The next morning, Samantha had woken him a few minutes before the bus normally came to pick up children at the bus stop. She wanted to know what time it was. Realizing it was late, he'd instructed her to hurry so as not to miss the bus. It was the last time he'd seen her. She was wearing a purple jacket and carrying a Disney backpack. She hadn't been on the bus for the return trip home that afternoon, and he had no idea where Samantha was.

After walking Colon back to the trailer, the investigator next questioned Rachel. Her sequence of events was much the same as Colon's. Having fallen asleep watching TV with her young daughters, Angel had awakened her around 11:30, telling her to go to bed. She hadn't seen Samantha that morning because she hadn't been feeling well and had slept late. Her assumption was that Samantha had been in school when she and Angel took the two toddlers to preschool on Main Street in Perry around 8:30 AM. The couple had collected bread and some other free groceries from the nearby Presbyterian Church. They'd gone on to Batavia and Warsaw, running several errands. Rachel had no idea Samantha was missing until later in the afternoon around 3:15 or 3:30 PM.

Results of interviews with the neighbors were reported to the investigative team. Children who rode the bus with Samantha said she hadn't gotten on the bus that morning. No one had seen her in the driveway or walking to the bus stop. Rachel's father, Bruno Stra, who lived across the road with his girlfriend, Lisa Johnson, hadn't seen Samantha either. But people had seen other things the evening before. Living in proximity of each other, neighbors saw and heard the comings and goings of all the families in the mobile home park.

After interviewing the couple and considering the statements of the neighbors, the undersheriff and investigator agreed they needed to question Colon further. The investigators had also noted that neither Angel nor Rachel showed signs of much emotional upset. Ely returned to the trailer and asked Colon if he was willing to ride to Warsaw and be interviewed further at the sheriff's office. Colon had no objections.

I arrived a little before 8:30 PM to process evidence in the trailer. Sheriff Capwell was present and brought me up to date on the investigation. Colon was with the undersheriff and Investigator Spink for more questioning at the sheriff's office in Warsaw. The evidence to be collected was in the bedroom where the three girls slept. A set of bunk beds filled a good portion of the small room. Rachel had located the clothing Samantha had worn on the previous day, which was a pair of underpants, a long-sleeved shirt, and pants. We secured a Disney *Aladdin* shirt and two other pieces of clothing, and then we spotted a white print blanket on the top bunk where Samantha slept. Several small red stains were evident on it. Undersheriff Ely had previously asked Rachel what the stains might be. She thought the marks were most likely makeup. She'd explained that her daughters were drawn to their mother's cosmetics and enjoyed playing with them. After photographing the room, clothing, and blanket, I secured the items in my vehicle for the return to the sheriff's office. I would place them in the evidence room later that evening.

The mobile home park had been an active beehive for several hours. There was the real possibility Samantha had been snatched right outside her home in broad daylight. That frightening scenario meant the FBI would join the investigation very soon.

Spink and Ely sat down in the interview room at 7:50 PM with Angel Colon and advised him of his rights. Colon agreed to talk to the men without an attorney present, and they began to go over the events of Tuesday and Wednesday once again. Colon answered the questions, and when asked if he would take a Computer Voice Stress Analyzer (CVSA) test, he agreed. The Livingston County Sheriff's Office (LCSO) would administer the test since they had the equipment, and arrangements were quickly made for the test to be given at 10:00 PM that night. Colon hesitated, requesting that the appointment be made for the following morning. The appointment was immediately changed, and Investigator Herkimer of the LCSO was scheduled to administer the test at 9:00 AM, Thursday. The interview ended, and Colon followed the investigator out to the parking lot to get a ride home.

CHAPTER 3

Thursday, February 27, 1997

The report that first grader Samantha Zaldivar was missing hit the front page of *The Daily News*, the area's afternoon newspaper, located in Batavia, NY. At a morning news conference with Sheriff Capwell, he asked for anyone with information about the disappearance to contact Undersheriff Ely. The sheriff assured everyone that any information given would be kept confidential. He told reporters that there were no leads yet and he refused to speculate on the possibility of foul play. It was very early in the investigation, and there was much work to do.

Gary Almeter, fire chief of the Gainesville Fire Department, offered more information on the search for Samantha, which had ramped up since being suspended around midnight the previous night. A NYS Police helicopter was assisting those on the ground. Members of the Massasauga Search and Rescue Team and their dogs joined the fifty to sixty volunteers, forest rangers, sheriff's department personnel, and state troopers. The search would once again concentrate on a half-mile to three-quarter-mile radius around the trailer park. The weather was miserable—a windy, rainy, and cold day, making the job more difficult for those involved. The helicopter was forced to land early because of high winds as searchers on the ground continued to hunt for any sign of Samantha.

Angel Colon was on his way to Geneseo for the CVSA test, as was Investigator Spink. Once at the Livingston

County Sheriff's Office in Geneseo, NY, Colon signed a Miranda Warning and Truth Verification Release form before the test was administered.

Law enforcement sometimes prefers the Computer Voice Stress Analysis test over a polygraph because it only requires the CVSA software on a laptop and a microphone. Like the polygraph, it isn't admissible in court but can be a valuable tool in determining whether someone is being deceptive. Investigators needed some direction, and they felt the CVSA was the means to assist them.

Voice analysis research began in the late 1950s when tiny, involuntary tremors in a muscle were discovered in times of stress. Based on the "flight or fight" reaction, voice analyzers can identify stress in a subject's speech. These small frequency modulations in the voice appear when someone is lying.

Investigator Martin Herkimer, who was trained to give and interpret the findings of the CVSA test, sat down with Colon. The investigator began with simple yes-and-no questions, establishing a baseline of reactions. He started with, "Is your name Angel Colon?"

"Yes," stated Colon.

After a series of similar questions, Herkimer asked, "Did you leave your residence in the Bronco you drive after midnight on Tuesday night, early Wednesday morning?"

Colon responded, "No."

Herkimer continued with his set of fifteen questions, watching the computer screen. After the test was completed, he examined the results, sharing them with Investigators Spink and Eck. The investigators decided to re-administer the test, and then it was given to Colon for a third time, each round of testing with the same exact questions. The results of three tests were identical. Colon's responses indicated deception, which warranted another interview. Colon continued to be cooperative and also signed a consent allowing them to search the 1988 Bronco.

I was back in Hermitage on Thursday morning at 10:00 to meet with Undersheriff Ely, who directed me to meet Trooper Tim Talley on Hermitage Road. A small pet cemetery had been discovered to the north of the trailer park, and there appeared to have been some recent burials. The soil was of a different color in one of the burial spots, which had caught Talley's attention. We located and spoke with the landowner, Lyle Drake, who gave us permission to check out the area. The wind was icy as we bent over the wet mound of dirt and carefully dug out a plastic garbage bag. We breathed a sigh of relief. The remains of a dog were in the bag, and after checking out the section once more, we left. There was still the chance that Samantha was alive.

By 1:30 PM, I'd been advised that I was needed in Geneseo to collect evidence from a 1988 Bronco, which Investigator Spink had secured. I had also learned that the FBI was sending an evidence response team to assist. Special Agent Timothy Crino, Agents Daphne Hearn, and Rob Lewis would aid us in the collection of evidence.

Deputy Mike Hildreth of the Monroe County Sheriff's Office was also on his way and would meet us in Geneseo with an Alternate Light Source (ALS). This technology would prove invaluable as the investigation rapidly pressed forward. Budgets were tight in Wyoming County, and although I'd lobbied for the purchase of an ALS, the price tag was too much for our equipment budget. It was difficult to make headway with the Board of Supervisors when the piece of equipment resembled a flashlight but cost more than $12,000. Even with the support of the sheriff and undersheriff, the ALS wouldn't be purchased until after we had closed the Zaldivar case. The demonstration I gave less than a year later to members of the Public Safety Committee of the Wyoming County Board of Supervisors about the proven value of an ALS in this case finally sealed the deal.

The search of the Bronco began in the late afternoon and ended seven hours later. Thirty-seven pieces of evidence were taken from the vehicle and secured by the FBI. Investigators painstakingly combed the vehicle so as not to miss anything. A stain was discovered on the front seat on the passenger side of the SUV. It appeared to be blood. The standard procedure, using a cotton swab dipped in distilled water and then touching a Hemastix®, was conducted.

A Hemastix® is designed to determine if iron is present, and the test read negative after several tries. The stain was still suspect, and we would find a better way to test the area later on. A thirty-eighth piece of evidence would be taken from the vehicle when it arrived at the Wyoming County Sheriff's Office a little after 10:00 PM on a flatbed truck. Special Agent Tim Crino and I cut out a section of the Bronco's carpet on the passenger side. The carpet was wet, and an empty can of "Tuff Stuff" (a multi-purpose foam cleaner) had been found on the carpet. We secured the items and placed them in the sheriff's evidence room. Then I was back on the road to Colon and Stra's residence, arriving at 11:35 PM. The FBI evidence response team, along with Captain Michael Melton and Mike Griffin of the Amherst Police Department, were finishing their collection of evidence at the trailer, which would yield twenty-two items.

Special Agent Crino had put in a call to Captain Melton to help with photographing the evidence at the trailer. Melton had photographic expertise in low-light situations, and his department had an ALS. Even the FBI didn't have ALS at the time, and Crino knew the technology would be needed to do the job right. I had a great mentor in Tim Crino. A special agent with the FBI since 1985, he had investigated many high-profile cases, including TWA Flight 800 that exploded and crashed into the Atlantic on July 17, 1996. He would go on to investigate the bombings of the *USS Cole* and the World Trade Center. Tim served almost thirty years with the FBI and today is the Director of Lakelet Financial Forensics Group and a sought-after speaker on forensics.

Evidence collection is an exacting process and was my primary responsibility as a Technical Sergeant. I worked alongside the FBI team, following the protocols to ensure that the items collected were properly documented, collected, packaged, and preserved. Gloves, protective clothing, and the use of any other protective equipment if necessary were essential in the collection of evidence. We needed to safeguard the gathering of every item so it would meet the legal and scientific requirements for admissibility in a court of law. Failure to do so could result in questions about the origin of the evidence and cross-contamination between items collected; additionally the evidence could also decompose or deteriorate.

When first arriving at the scene, each piece of evidence must be photographed before it is touched, moved, or collected. The location and condition of the object must be documented. The crime scene is sketched, and the drawing includes evidence and objects relative to the crime scene. Then the items are collected in an appropriate manner, dependent upon what they are. It's a time-consuming process, requiring attention to detail and patience. Television shows compress these extensive procedures into less than an hour for our entertainment. Their miniscule window of time is far from reality. Hours, days, and even weeks are required to collect, test, and evaluate evidence.

There are hundreds of varieties of physical evidence commonly submitted to forensic crime laboratories by law enforcement agencies. DNA (deoxyribonucleic acid) analysis of evidence is generally limited to substances which are biological in nature. Materials most often tested are: hair with follicles, tissues and cells, semen and seminal stains, blood and bloodstains, bones, organs, saliva, and urine.

The eight-member FBI team was working with Melton and Griffin of the Amherst PD when I arrived on scene. The small trailer was full of people, and the tiny bedroom the girls slept in had room for only two or three to work at a time. ADA David Di Matteo was outside in his vehicle, available to answer any questions the team might have. DA Stout was attending a conference in New York City and the ADA was also keeping him informed while the search continued. Di Matteo was shuttling to and from Rowe's store to talk with the DA. The phone booth there was in constant use during the investigation. Cell phone signals were intermittent as were our radios. The county was infamous for many communication dead spots because of the terrain. The Hermitage area was one of those spots.

The first twenty-four hours of feverish activity had drawn in numerous outside agencies, the community, and the entire personnel of the WCSO. We needed evidence to determine what kind of case we were dealing with. Was Samantha visiting friends? Had she been abducted? Was she with relatives, or had she been murdered? All these questions remained unanswered. We were fortunate to have outside law enforcement agencies step up and assist us with manpower and technology. Without them, we wouldn't have accomplished so much in this short period of time.

The addition of the FBI Evidence Response Team was irreplaceable. Agents, technicians, and equipment were brought in to help in any way they were needed. From the start, there was never a feeling that they were taking over or looking down on our department. We were all there to find Samantha, and everyone focused on the task at hand. It would not be easy, and answers were difficult to find. Even in the search of the trailer, things would be trying.

Just a little more than two hours into the search, the electricity went off in the trailer, which slowed the team's progress. The extreme windy weather had taken out electricity all over the county that day. When it appeared the power was going to be off for a length of time, a generator was requested, which took another ninety minutes before it was connected to restore some of the lights.

After the generator was operational, Captain Melton used his department's ALS, which could expose stains that were invisible to the naked eye. Stains were discovered on a bunkbed rail, a wall in the hallway, and a rug in the hall. Each tested positive for blood. The team used flashlights to search so as not to overlook anything in the poorly-lit mobile home.

Blankets, small pieces of mattress foam, wallpaper, and a towel with possible bloodstains were documented and collected. Items from every part of the home were examined, including damp bathroom rugs hanging from the railing of the back porch. SA Crino decided to take the entire bedrail as evidence.

Deputies and investigators not involved with the search were interviewing every possible witness to flesh out the events of the previous few days. Establishing a timeline of Samantha's activities up to the moment of her disappearance was vital. Law enforcement focused on Letchworth Central School District personnel, specifically questioning the Lockwood Elementary School principal, teachers, bus driver, and friends of Samantha about her disappearance. The school administration notified classmates and other students that she was missing. Everyone was shaken that such a thing could happen in this rural school district. Pieces of information began to fill in the blanks as the day progressed. Samantha's bus driver Sam Zanghi was certain she hadn't gotten on or off his bus on February 26. Her friends hadn't seen her in school that day, and her teachers had marked her absent.

Samantha was part of the Primary House class, which combined first and second grades. Her entrance into school after the family's move to Hermitage from Florida was difficult. Rachel hadn't provided any records of Samantha attending kindergarten when she and Angel enrolled her at Lockwood Elementary. Samantha attended summer school and scored well enough on the kindergarten screening to convince the principal to place her in the combined grade, although it appeared to school officials she would have been more suited to kindergarten. Samantha's teachers described the quiet, dark-haired girl as withdrawn and in need of additional help. She tended to be clingy with certain people at school, seeking affection. Her attendance had been sporadic, causing problems with her school work.

At the school's request, Wyoming County Department of Social Services (WCDSS) became involved earlier in the school year to give assistance to the family. Rachel seemed frustrated with parenting her oldest daughter, and the WCDSS stepped in to help. A Home Health Aide and Preventative Services Worker were assigned to assist Rachel with tips on helping with homework and managing her home. Her teachers and the principal noted that the last few weeks before February 26, Samantha was increasingly tardy and absent from school. Her personal appearance had altered as well. Her clothing and personal hygiene had declined; she seemed unkempt. As the FBI investigators probed further, one of her teachers commented that in her opinion, the child was incapable of running away. She was heavily dependent upon adults, and it seemed improbable to her that the child would take the initiative to hide from anyone or actually run away from home.

Although the school office had called the trailer trying to reach Stra on Wednesday to inquire about Samantha's absence, no one was home. The principal, Adele Bovard, had urged Rachel to call the police when she had contacted the school office that afternoon, looking for Samantha. The mother had taken the advice, and Colon had made the call to the WCSO. School officials were sick at heart, trying to remember any detail that would lead law enforcement to the little girl.

Tips were coming in by phone and other means. Two pedophiles lived within three miles of Hermitage Meadows Trailer Court, and investigators were quick to interview the men. Both accounted for their whereabouts at the time of Samantha's disappearance. It was an abrupt dead end, and investigators moved on after confirming the men's alibis.

Bruno Stra, Samantha's grandfather, and his fiancée Lisa Johnson were interviewed; neighbors were re-interviewed. Rachel Stra was questioned again about the events leading up to the disappearance.

Rachel's family in Florida was hearing about Samantha's disappearance, as was Noel Zaldivar, her biological father. It was then that Rachel learned of his telephone call with their daughter over the Christmas holidays when Samantha had gone to visit her grandmother in Florida. She expressed immediate concern that Noel could have taken his daughter. Ruth Velarde, Rachel's mother, made arrangements to fly to New York. Alexandria Suarez, Rachel's sister, and her husband would travel with Ruth. The family was in shock. Only several weeks prior, Ruth's granddaughter had shared the Christmas holiday with her. They'd even talked about Samantha coming to live with her. Now, she wanted answers.

CHAPTER 4

Friday, February 28, 1997

The answers law enforcement had gleaned only generated more questions in the twenty-four-hour time period, with more interviews and more searches. Angel and Rachel's timeline of events following Samantha's disappearance had to be followed up. Colon's accounts were not quite matching. Details of the evening before the disappearance and Wednesday morning kept shifting. Tips were also coming in, which had to be checked out by investigators and the FBI. As investigators reviewed interviews with neighbors, school employees, and county workers, they knew they had much more work to do. Eyes were on Angel Colon, but so far nothing definitive had connected the twenty-three-year-old man to the little girl's disappearance. He insisted that he had not harmed Samantha and had sent her to school the morning of February 26.

The Zaldivar, Stra, and Colon families had an abundance of background information on the couple and the three girls. All were willing to talk, especially Samantha's biological father, Noel Zaldivar. He had been notified of Samantha's disappearance by his ex-mother-in-law and was eager to assist with the investigation. He accounted for his whereabouts, and it quickly became evident he hadn't been in New York State. Twenty-seven years old, Noel Zaldivar had spoken with his daughter in January 1997, after several years of silence. He had last seen Samantha in 1993. At her maternal grandmother's prompting, Samantha had called her father in Mexico while staying at Velarde's home in Florida over the Christmas break. Zaldivar told the FBI she had seemed fine and understood that he was her real father. He was anxious to distribute photos of his daughter and travel to New York to help with the search.

Bruno Stra, Rachel's father and Samantha's grandfather, and his girlfriend Lisa Johnson cooperated from the start. Lisa had spotted Angel exiting a shed in her backyard, and then he'd come to the door Wednesday afternoon. Lisa was surprised at his odd demeanor and that he was holding Samantha's cat. She'd never seen the cat outside, and it had never crossed the road to her house before. After that day, the cat would become a regular visitor to her yard and would disappear into the woods behind the property.

Her own children were still at school and expected home on the late bus, so she told him to check to see if Samantha was staying late too. It wasn't long after Angel left that Lisa received a call from Rachel. The school had informed Rachel that Samantha had been absent that day. Lisa quickly checked her telephone message machine to see if there was a call from the school about the absence since she and Bruno were additional family contacts. There was no message from the school.

Her children were now home, and they hadn't seen Samantha that day either. They were positive she hadn't been on the morning bus. Lisa's son and daughter began inspecting the property for any place that Samantha might be hiding. Bruno arrived home a few minutes later from picking up his vehicle at a friend's house. He immediately went to see Rachel to find out what was going on.

The SAR dogs were later sent to search the area around their property that sat across the road from the trailer court owned by Lisa. No trace of Samantha was found either by scent, footprint, nor was there any other clue as to her whereabouts.

Bruno, who identified himself as a private investigator, had urged Rachel to move from Florida to the rural area in hopes that his daughter would improve her lifestyle and provide a safer environment for his grandchildren. The original arrangement was for Rachel and the three girls to live in the trailer. When Lisa and Bruno met the family's red vehicle on Route 390 and Route 15 the previous year, Angel had been in the car. Displeased that Colon was with his daughter, Bruno finally relented, and it was decided Angel could stay. Bruno had loaned his Ford Bronco to Angel and Rachel so that they would have transportation since Angel's vehicle, a red sports car, had apparently been repossessed late one night shortly after the family moved into the trailer. He'd even sent significant amounts of money to Rachel and Noel in previous years to help with Samantha's financial support. He immediately offered his help to the police to find his granddaughter.

According to Samantha's relatives, Angel had been with Rachel on and off since 1991 when he'd met her in North Miami. Drugs and stealing to feed his crack cocaine habit had caused problems in the relationship, and Rachel had her own issues with drugs. He'd moved to Georgia at one point to continue his habitual drug use, even stealing from his mother to get high.

The volatile relationship between the couple had been reestablished, and taking the opportunity to find steady work away from the frenetic culture of Miami, the family moved to Western New York. Lisa was allowing them to live in the trailer. If they made payments on it, the title for the trailer would be registered in Rachel's name once they had paid in full. Lisa wasn't even charging the family for renting the lot to help them out. Despite the struggles with her relationship with Colon, and parenting three small girls, Rachel was taking courses at Genesee Community College in the hopes of bettering herself.

It appeared they had not really settled into life in a rural setting. Both Rachel and Angel kept to themselves and didn't seem to have friends. However, their children played with several children in the trailer park, and Samantha had a birthday party a month earlier. A few school friends stayed overnight to celebrate with her.

The school district's intervention had prompted help from the Wyoming Area Homemakers, Inc. They had been referred by the Wyoming County Department of Social Services (WCDSS) to assist Rachel and Angel. The parent aide, Martha Wilson*, had been assigned to the home for several months, with twice-a-week visits. It was evident to Wilson that Rachel and Samantha did not get along. In fact, Rachel had difficulty holding any conversation with her children without yelling. Rachel admitted to a lack of patience with her daughters, especially Samantha. The majority of the home visits were during school hours, and Wilson hadn't seen the seven-year-old very often. When she did, the girl was quiet and reserved, but often acted as a "little mama" to her younger sisters.

The strife in the family wasn't hidden, and there had been talk of Angel leaving in March to return to Florida to find work. He was angry and frustrated. Rachel was determined to stay in New York to continue college classes. The parent aide had observed other peculiar events in the home, including an incident over some unopened birthday presents. Samantha asked Wilson if she could open some of the birthday presents she hadn't been allowed to open on her birthday. When Rachel returned to the home later, she became very upset, yelling at her oldest daughter for opening the presents. It was a complete mystery to the aide why the child wasn't able to have her birthday presents.

Noel's sister, Lucely Zaldivar, shared information about Samantha and her family. She had continued to stay in touch with her niece and wanted to make sure she was treated well and wasn't in danger. The Zaldivar family considered Angel Colon to be unpredictable and violent. Her brother's marriage to Rachel had gone badly; a string of affairs, drugs, and domestic violence had marked the couple's time together. Noel had separated from Rachel and had gone back to Mexico at one point. He'd returned to try and make a go of it with Rachel without success. Angel Colon was in her life. There were stories of Angel using a baseball bat on a new car given to Rachel by her mother. It was her punishment for leaving and trying to hide from him. Samantha had been a witness to and a victim of a constant barrage of domestic abuse, drugs, and instability. She'd been instructed to keep quiet about what she saw and how she was treated.

Rachel's sister Alexandria and their mother Ruth painted a very similar picture of Stra and Colon's relationship when they lived in Florida. The reality of the little girl's home life was emerging, making investigators work even harder to dig out the truth. Evidence was the key, and it would take time to obtain the results. But the spotlight was back on Colon and Stra, who were interviewed at the sheriff's office. At the conclusion of the questioning, they were asked to take polygraph tests the next day in in Batavia, New York. Both agreed.

On February 28, the couple was taken to Batavia. Angel had second thoughts about taking the polygraph once he arrived at the troopers' headquarters and refused. According to Rachel, he was feeling the scrutiny of law enforcement and began to back away from cooperating. He'd commented that if law enforcement officials suspected him, they would make sure he failed the polygraph. Rachel was visibly upset by his refusal and responded that if he didn't take the lie detector test on the next testing date, which was March 3, she'd believe that he was involved with Samantha's disappearance.

Rachel herself had no qualms and went ahead with the test, which was administered by the New York State Police. She passed the test, while Angel stubbornly declined when asked a second time.

The polygraph test, commonly known as the lie detector test, measures physical reactions to questions. The test was developed in 1921 by John Larson, a medical student at the University of California. Blood pressure and respirations are measured, as is skin conductivity, which is related to the sweat response as the interviewee supplies answers to the polygraphist's questions. Like the Computer Voice Analysis test, the results aren't admissible in court, but are often used to determine if a subject is lying. Despite its detractors, the tool is a standard in criminal investigations.

While Angel and Rachel were in Batavia, the ground search for Samantha continued, with volunteers making up the majority of searchers. There was still no sign of the little girl, and then a telephone tip came in to the sheriff's department. A resident in the Hermitage area had observed a red color in the ice on his pond. It looked like blood to him.

Once again, outside agencies with personnel and equipment came to assist the sheriff's department. Batavia City Police and the Genesee County Sheriff's Office provided scuba divers to search the pond. Patrick Corona of the Batavia PD and Investigator John Dehm of GCSO expected the worse as they went into the frigid water in their scuba gear. After they meticulously searched the murky pond and removed their masks, a mix of relief and disappointment was on their faces. They had found no sign of Samantha.

The volume of leads from the public prompted Undersheriff Ely to place a strict gag order on any information about the case. The sheriff, undersheriff, and only five others—members of the investigative team—had access to anything in connection with the case that was entered into the sheriff's database. The department wanted to avoid any leaks to the media and kept everything close to the vest.

Swamped with leads to follow, the FBI sent about fifty agents to help manage them all. They set up a command center in a meeting room at the sheriff's office. Computers, modems, printers, faxes—all kinds of equipment stood on the tables, and the agents immediately joined us in tracking down people and information. Without their help, we would have been drowning in work. Everyone hoped that some tip would come in to solve the case quickly.

CHAPTER 5

Saturday, March 1, 1997

After three days of an exhaustive ground search with an army of community volunteers, fireman, and law enforcement, the search effort was significantly scaled back. No sign of Samantha had been found anywhere in the two-mile radius around the mobile home park. It seemed she had vanished into thin air. Investigators and searchers were frustrated with the absence of any sign of the young girl in the vicinity. But telephone callers were leaving daily tips, and investigators continued to re-interview neighbors and family members. They were combing every report for any bit of information that would lead to finding Samantha.

Anne Trevitt*, a neighbor of Stra and Colon, was on her way to take a polygraph in Batavia. Her statement regarding Colon's activities in the wee hours of Wednesday, February 26 was significant. Trevitt* was laid off from her job at Champion Products in Perry, just as Colon was. Her daughter, Miranda Trevitt*, was a friend of Samantha's, and they played regularly together. They also rode the same school bus. Anne had experienced trouble sleeping since the layoff and had gotten into the habit of watching TV until late at night. She'd been dozing while watching television on Tuesday night, and she awoke at 11:45 PM. Switching off the TV, she began reading near a window where she had a good view of the entrance to the trailer park and Hermitage Road. At 1:30 AM, Colon's Ford Bronco drove out of the trailer park, turning left onto Hermitage Road. The Bronco returned at 2:50 AM, coming from the same direction. She was certain of the times, since she'd checked the clock at the departure and arrival. Trevitt was positive the vehicle was Colon's, although she couldn't see who was driving, or if there was a passenger. After the polygraph was given at the NYS Police station, the results indicated that she was truthful. But we still needed more information. Angel Colon was adamant he hadn't left the residence Tuesday night or early Wednesday morning.

A deluge of community responses came into the sheriff's office after our pleas for any tidbit that could help us find Samantha. We received hundreds of possible leads in the first three days of the case. All had to be checked out quickly and thoroughly. Investigators were constantly on the run to keep up with them and handle normal county business as well. There were no days off for anyone, and we were feeling overwhelmed with the workload.

One phone tip led to a location in Allegany County, which warranted further investigation. A flurry of calls was made to the Allegany County Sheriff, the NYS Troopers in Wellsville, and the FBI Response Team to inform them of our lead. Sheriff Capwell, Investigator David Davis, and I went to Pond Road in the Town of Hume. The area was in the Mills' Mill area near Wiscoy Creek, remote farmland with thick woods.

Just off the muddy roadway in the leaves was an eight-inch circle covered with a thick, red substance that looked like blood. There were also several glass fragments that appeared to be from a vehicle. My preliminary testing at the site confirmed it was blood. Whether it was human or animal was a question we needed answered swiftly.

After photographing the scene, I began to collect samples, which consisted of the bloody leaves, a soil sample from underneath the leaves, and a pair of purple panties that were discovered across the road. The blood evidence was wet and a cause for concern. If it was covered, mold could quickly contaminate the sample. Strands of hair were also present in the blood, which needed to be identified.

A call was made to Monroe County Undersheriff Patrick O'Flynn, who immediately gave us the help needed. O'Flynn contacted Thomas Rodwell, the Laboratory Director for the Monroe County Public Safety Crime Lab in Rochester, NY. The director was willing to meet me at the lab to examine and test the samples that night.

Knocking on the door of the crime lab around 8:00 PM, I identified myself to Tom Rodwell when he opened the door. He had generously opened up the facility just to assist in the investigation. I signed in at a desk near the entrance and followed him back into the lab area. The harsh fluorescent lights overhead lit up a room that reminded me of a high school science room with multiple worktables, microscopes, lights, and other equipment. Tom and I went to work immediately, carefully pulling the pieces of hair from the blood with tweezers to be examined separately. He prepared slides of the blood and hair to study under the microscope. A delicate process, just setting up the collected evidence for his testing would take several hours. But late that night, we had the results. The blood was determined to be feline in origin, and the hairs we had separated from the blood were established as animal hair. Although the scene was odd, and even suspicious, it was in no way connected to the Zaldivar case. Our hopes were raised that this might prove to be a real clue to finding Samantha. Unfortunately, it was another dead end.

While I was engaged with the evidence collection in Allegany County, Noel Zalidvar and his sister Lucely arrived at the Buffalo airport. The brother and sister found lodging at a Warsaw motel for the next four days. They met with Undersheriff Ely and others involved in the investigation, and both promised to help law enforcement in any way. They had flyers to distribute and were eager to talk with the press about Samantha's disappearance. Although Noel had been estranged from his daughter for five years, he was focused on disseminating as much information about his missing daughter as possible. He went to work to gain more publicity on the case, contacting the Spanish television station Univision about their plight. A television crew was on site in the village of Warsaw within two days. Originating in New York City, the show, *Primer Impacto* (*First Impact*), would feature the story. The program was similar to the then popular *Hard Copy* TV show, and a segment on missing children was a part of the show's format.

During the time Noel Zaldivar was in Wyoming County, he gave blood samples, which became another item of evidence in the search.

Days were full, especially in that first week of the investigation. I also continued to work on the fire investigation of a mobile home on February 13 that had claimed the lives of a mother and her two children in the Town of Perry. Every case had to be handled properly, and all of them demanded our attention and time. We couldn't ignore all others to focus exclusively on Samantha. Effective time management was essential, and we had to divide our working hours between cases in order to make progress on any of them. The capable assistance of the FBI in the first weeks of Samantha's disappearance facilitated the rapid collection of evidence and statements that were fundamental in finding the truth of what had really happened to her.

CHAPTER 6

Sunday, March 2 – Monday, March 3, 1997

Residents in the trailer park had witnessed two key events that led to a more intense scrutiny of Colon's movements the evening of Tuesday, February 25 and the early morning hours of Wednesday, February 26. Besides observing the Bronco, a neighbor who lived next door to the Stra and Colon residence heard a piercing scream the evening of Tuesday, February 25. Ada Fuller thought she'd heard a child scream, hearing it over the sound of her television. Lowering the volume, she waited, but heard nothing more. Loud arguments and noise coming from the trailer weren't unusual, she said. She was hesitant to say more.

Lisa had spoken to Samantha on Tuesday night. The seven-year-old had called to ask if Jenna, Lisa's nine-year-old daughter, could spend the night. Lisa hadn't allowed the sleepover because it was a school night. Samantha then told her that she had an earache. Lisa advised her to have her mother give her some Tylenol, not realizing that Rachel was at school.

Wyoming County Investigator Dennis Spink and Investigator Paul Donnelly were on their way to Williamsville, a small village outside of Buffalo. They were transporting Rachel, her two daughters, Bruno Stra, and Parental Aide Martha Wilson* to meet with child psychologist Dr. William Condrell. Concern was growing over the safety of the two little girls. Had they witnessed something in the home or somewhere else?

Investigator Gary Eck was interviewing Noel Zaldivar and his sister Lucely. One of the primary questions was if Noel knew Samantha's blood type. He didn't, but provided information about the Miami hospital in which she was born. He also knew she'd had received immunizations at the HRS Health Office in Miami. Noel agreed to give a blood sample and went to the Wyoming County Community Hospital with Eck.

Monday, March 3, 1997

FBI Agent Larry Wack and I headed to Letchworth Central School to re-interview Samantha's teachers and the elementary principal. We covered the same ground about the family, Samantha's appearance, her demeanor, and her friends. Any tidbit of information overlooked in previous interviews might be of value. District Superintendent Dr. Joseph Backer handed us the items from Samantha's cubby locker while we sat in Principal Bovard's office. White sneakers, a Tweety Bird sweatshirt, and a pair of small gloves made up the entire contents. Once again, school officials repeated their impressions that Samantha's appearance had deteriorated over the last three weeks she'd been in school. One of her teachers described a phonics book that should have been in her backpack. She'd been given an assignment to complete the day before her disappearance.

Residents in the trailer park were being re-interviewed, as was Lucely Zaldivar. She described her encounter with Rachel and Angel, the first night she and Noel were in Wyoming County. Bruno Stra had driven the pair to the trailer park for the visit. Noel stayed in the car with Bruno, avoiding any contact with Angel. Lucely entered the trailer and found an exhausted Rachel, who could barely keep her eyes open, while Angel was "pumped up." He was very vocal about the spotlight on him as a suspect. Rachel kept repeating, "This wasn't supposed to happen to us." She went on to say that Samantha had her very first friend, and the family was happy. But she was worried that everyone thought Angel was involved. Rubbing her temples, Rachel sat on the couch, while Angel continued to pace.

Lucely tried to convince Angel he needed to submit to the polygraph to clear things up. But the Hispanic man answered that he'd taken the test twice, and he was considering hiring a lawyer. If he took another lie detector test, it would be his last. He was sick of the police and their suspicions. He knew how to raise children, because he'd raised nieces and nephews back in Florida. However, in reality, Angel had twice refused to take a polygraph test, and he would quickly retain D. Michael Murray, Esq. of Batavia to represent him.

The rest of the neighbors in the trailer park had different levels of interaction with the three little girls, their mother, and Colon. Some indicated the girls were very quiet when they played outside and never heard fighting or loud conversations from the trailer. Others had witnessed Colon and Stra arguing angrily with Bruno outside the residence. No one had ever seen either Colon or Stra hit their children in their home or outside.

Miranda Trevitt*, Samantha's friend, spoke of Angel's affection for Samantha. He often hugged her, but had strict rules about behavior inside. No slamming of doors, no running, or jumping. She'd seen Samantha violate the rules, and Angel had punished her by sending the girl to her room. Miranda and Samantha played together often, sometimes at Miranda's and other times at Samantha's home. She hadn't noticed any difference in Samantha over the past few months, but did know that her younger friend often missed the bus. She also fell asleep on the bus, which had happened the afternoon of February 25.

After almost a week of interviews, an intensive search, and following up leads that led us everywhere in the area, hope was dim that we would find Samantha alive. The pressure was on Angel Colon, and it was about to get worse.

CHAPTER 7

Tuesday, March 4, 1997

The *Primer Impacto* crew was in Warsaw interviewing Samantha's family and law enforcement. It was a circus-like atmosphere in the county seat with TV cameras, reporters, equipment vans, and community members gathering to see what was going on. There was an icy edge to the breeze, and the sky was slate gray as people bundled up in coats, hats, and gloves stood on the sidewalk in front of the courthouse. Noel and Lucely Zaldivar talked with the media.

There were a few snow flurries in the air as I drove down NYS Route 19 South to jump onto Interstate 490 East to get to the crime lab in Rochester, arriving around 9:30 AM to meet once again with the director, Tom Rodwell. We were waiting for Special Agent Crino, who was bringing the evidence that had been secured in the FBI offices in Buffalo. The items were from the search of the trailer and the Bronco. Walking out to the parking lot, I saw Crino's car pull in and helped him carry the evidence bags and containers into the lab. We had blue and pink bathroom rugs taken from the railings of the back steps, a blanket from the master bedroom, a piece of wallpaper, a Buffalo Bills coat that Angel often wore, sections of carpet, a piece of the bunkbed where Samantha slept, and pieces of a foam mattress. Many of these items contained traces of blood, and we needed to find out whose blood it was. After logging each piece into the lab records, we handed them over to forensic chemist Harvey VanHoven for analysis.

While I was in Rochester, FBI agents sat down with sheriff's investigators for an intensive meeting to sort out leads and compare notes. Their Miami division was in the process of interviewing relatives of Angel and Rachel, hoping to catch some sort of break with new information. One conclusion that the agents had already reached was that Rachel had gone to school Tuesday evening just as she had told investigators. She'd signed in for her class at 6:00 PM and left at 9:00 PM. Classmates, the professor, and school personnel had seen her come to class and leave. It was a thirty-minute drive each way, which squared with her timeline. She'd also passed the lie detector test given to her on February 28.

The couple's activities on Wednesday, February 26 had been followed up, as agents attempted to confirm previous statements. They knew the parents had dropped off Cassandra and Angela at the preschool in Perry and then traveled to Batavia where Angel had purchased a Corrections Officer book at Sleight's Bookstore to prepare for the state test. It was also confirmed he'd stopped in at the DMV in Warsaw where he was issued a temporary license. A DMV employee remembered the transaction, but not the time. Angel's name had been misspelled on his permit, and he was in the process of correcting the error.

The Genesee Community College professor who taught Rachel's evening class had informed agents that his own children rode the same bus as Samantha. They hadn't seen her get on the bus on February 26. Although he didn't personally know Rachel, the professor had contacted the home to express his sympathy over Samantha's disappearance. The call was answered by Angel, who seemed more concerned over the police questioning him and didn't focus on Samantha's disappearance.

The Human Resources department at Colon's former employer Champion confirmed his layoff date. The HR manager was able to tell Agent Mike Liwicki about the team Colon had worked on and some of the rumors in the facility of dating between the team members. In one of Rachel's interviews, she indicated that Angel had left their home late at night to see a woman a few times in the past. This was something they needed to know more about. Had Angel gone to see another woman Wednesday night while everyone was sleeping?

Interviews with pedophiles in the area continued, and plans were made to set up a polygraph test for one. Alibis needed confirmation, especially for the one who knew Samantha and other children in Hermitage Meadows Mobile Home Park.

Neighbors had seen the Bronco on the road on Wednesday, February 26. At one sighting, Rachel was the driver and only occupant. Most importantly, multiple individuals reported that Samantha hadn't been spotted that morning in the trailer park and hadn't been a passenger on the school bus.

The FBI team scheduled another interview with Rachel Stra at the Wyoming County Sheriff's Office. They also requested a blood sample from her, which she agreed to do at the hospital. Investigator Gary Eck escorted her to the hospital lab and secured three purple-topped tubes of blood, which were placed in the refrigerator in the sheriff's evidence room.

Once back at county offices, they rehashed the details of her relationships with Noel Zaldivar and Angel Colon. She talked further about discipline in the home, and because she judged herself too soft when it came to correcting her daughters, Angel was the disciplinarian. Guilt over her daughter's disappearance was growing because she hadn't gotten up to see her off to school. But it wasn't anything that was unusual. Samantha had her own alarm clock to wake her at 6:45 AM, while Rachel often slept past her own alarm that was set for 7:00 AM. She explained that was because of late nights studying for her classes.

The agents were also told that the couple didn't sleep together as a rule. The two younger girls regularly slept with their mother, with Angel on the couch, and Samantha in the top bunk in the girls' bedroom. Rachel recounted that Angel had experienced a recent nightmare brought on by Samantha's disappearance that she believed showed how upset he truly was.

The extensive interview with Dr. Condrell on March 2 with Angela and Cassandra was another topic the agents brought up. Rachel shared some of the details of the meeting in Williamsville. Angela, the three-year-old, told the psychologist she thought Samantha was dead and had been killed by a big boy, or maybe one of her girlfriends. Rachel also confided that she was beginning to believe Samantha was dead now after a week's time and no trace of her.

Rachel admitted to agents she hadn't asked her daughters about what had happened Wednesday night after she'd left for her evening class. She'd been confident that Samantha had left for school Thursday morning. Her focus had been on what had happened to her daughter after she went out the door of the trailer for the bus. Rachel stated over and over again, "This wasn't supposed to happen to us. We came here to be safe."

The dark-haired young woman pushed away from the table, looking at the door. She was finally done talking for the day. Rachel requested that the interview be discontinued, pleading fatigue and that she wanted to see her daughters, who were waiting for her at home with their father. The agents ended the questioning, and she headed back to Hermitage. There wouldn't be much family time that evening, however.

Wyoming County Social Services caseworkers, along with assistance from the sheriff's office, would soon knock on their door.

Sheriff's office vehicles swung into the circular driveway, accompanying the two caseworkers assigned to handle the case. Investigator Eck, Sergeant Linder, Investigator Donnelly, Deputy Perl, and I were assigned to assist. It was standard protocol for deputies to be present when children were to be removed immediately from their parents' care. The social workers never knew what kind of reaction they'd face. It had the potential to be violent and dangerous. We were expecting the worst.

Allegations of neglect of both Angela and Cassandra had been made against Rachel and Angel. The children were to be placed into foster care that night because there was reason to believe the girls were in a perilous environment. Caseworkers Debbie Vosburg and Dennis Huff made their way up the snowy wooden steps to the gray-colored trailer. Law enforcement officers were close behind. The door opened, and the group entered the trailer with the bad news. Social Services was taking the girls at that moment, pending more investigation into the allegations of neglect.

As expected, it didn't go well. Angel flew into a rage, arguing that his children were in no danger and we wouldn't take them "without a fight." He held Cassandra tightly in his arms. Rachel, shocked and emotional, seemed stunned at the news, as she looked at us and the social workers. There were no alternatives, insisted the caseworkers. The girls had to leave with them that night. They couldn't delay the removal. Angel continued to dispute their authority and the veracity of the charges. He wasn't going to allow anyone to lay a hand on his daughters and became physical in blocking the caseworkers from their sad task.

We worked to defuse the situation, explaining that the court would have to decide about the girls. The conversation went on for another half-hour. We didn't want anyone, especially the two little girls, to be hurt. The situation only worsened with Colon defiant, refusing to cooperate. We had to act, and looks were exchanged between Eck and me. Investigator Eck snatched Cassandra from her father's arms and handed her off to me. I stepped back to shield her while Eck and Linder took Colon to the floor, pinning him until the angry man was handcuffed. In seconds, Sergeant Linder took Angel into custody, arresting him for second-degree obstruction of governmental administration and resisting arrest. While the caseworkers put the preschoolers into their vehicle, Angel was placed in the back of a sheriff's car. Still angry, he was taken before the Town of Wethersfield Justice Elaine Skotnicki to be arraigned. Phone calls went to District Attorney Gerald Stout, Colon's attorney D. Michael Murray, and Undersheriff Ron Ely. DA Stout came to an agreement that night with Murray and Ely, allowing Angel to be released on his recognizance, with no bail required. A court date of March 17 was set by the justice to hear the misdemeanor charges. Little did we know that this incident would become key in the investigation.

Angel and Rachel returned to an empty home with a new set of problems. They now needed to concentrate on how to navigate the Family Court system to have their daughters returned to them.

CHAPTER 8

Wednesday, March 5, 1997

With no sightings of Samantha or credible leads to where she might be, new ideas were needed. Sheriff Capwell instructed me to head back to Hermitage Meadows at 3:00 PM to assist in a search of the septic tank that serviced the trailer park. It was another cold and snowy day, and I turned up my coat collar walking out past the Stra trailer to where the sheriff and several Gainesville firemen were standing. There were three manholes connected to the system, which were about forty yards from Samantha's home. The covers were about two feet in diameter and not locked. They weren't locked as a rule, and it would take only one person to remove a lid. Two were made from concrete, and the third manhole was covered with a wooden door. There was the real possibility that someone could easily dispose of a small body into the tank.

The Niagara County Sheriff's Department was represented by Special Deputy Bill Tolhurst, a cadaver dog handler accompanied by his two golden retrievers. Cadaver dogs are specifically trained to scent out the odor of blood and decaying human flesh. The body of a deceased person emits a unique smell, which is different than that of a dead animal. The unmistakable human scent is what the dogs are schooled to identify, even if the body is under rubble or underground. The retrievers wore red vests with a skull-and-crossbones badge on them and were already working the area around the septic tank. They kept noses to the ground, absorbed in their task. Fire department personnel hooked up a pump and tubing to empty eight feet of groundwater that lay in the tank. After the water had been drained, long poles were used to methodically search through the tank area, attempting to locate any indication of an object in the ground below. It was another unsuccessful search, but we were determined to leave no stone unturned in trying to find Samantha. We had pinned up one of the posters distributed in the area with her picture and physical description in the sheriff's office. Every day we took a hard look at the beautiful dark-haired, brown-eyed girl. We were all resolved to find her, and we couldn't fail.

Even though we came up empty once again in the trailer park, we decided to take the dogs and move out farther into the area, hoping to catch any break. Walking up through the snowy fields across from the trailer park, Tolhurst moved the two dogs through the frozen ground into the edge of the woods. After sweeping the area several times we called it a day. The dogs seemed baffled, and we felt the same.

Meanwhile, Rachel was working feverishly to regain custody of Angela and Cassandra. She retained her own lawyer, Antony N. Irrera, and he wasted no time in filing a petition with the Wyoming County Family Court to have the children returned to her. Rachel and her attorney stood before Wyoming County Family Court Judge Mark Dadd, waiting for his decision on the petition to return the girls to their mother. Judge Dadd determined that Rachel could have custody of her two young daughters if Angel Colon moved out of the residence. The DSS would also have to supervise any visits between Colon and his daughters. Rachel continued to support her fiancé, but she was now in a difficult position. He had to leave the home if she wanted to have her children back. Angel needed to find another place to live.

While the family court drama played out in Warsaw, Noel and Lucely Zaldivar were on their way back to Miami. After the previous day's media blitz, they'd decided there was nothing more they could do in Wyoming County to help find Samantha.

Thursday, March 6, 1997

Loading the seat taken from Colon's Bronco into the back of my county vehicle, a marked Chevy Suburban, I slid behind the wheel ready to take another trip to the crime lab in Rochester. The purple-topped tubes with blood samples from Noel Zaldivar and Rachel Stra were in a container on the front seat along with the carpet sample from the Bronco. We had yet to have any way to test for Samantha's blood, which was needed to compare to the collected items that contained traces of blood. The bloodstains on the mattress foam, rugs, wallpaper, and bunkbed needed to be identified.

The FBI continued field interviews, focusing on individuals who had worked with Colon at Champion. A picture of his personality and bits of his home life were revealed as coworkers recalled their encounters with the young Hispanic man. He liked flirting with women of all ages, and it appeared he enjoyed relationships with several women at the clothing manufacturing plant. His temper was notable, and he was not generally liked or trusted. He freely talked about slapping his oldest daughter to keep her in line. "She wasn't his real daughter" was another comment that he made often. Colon wasn't particularly fond of his neighbors because some had expressed concern about the three children being left alone. According to Colon, it wasn't anybody's business what he did. Investigators wrapped up the day's work, comparing notes and once again offering the polygraph test to Colon, who refused to take it upon advice from his attorney. Bruno had been pressuring Colon to take the test. If he truly hadn't harmed Samantha, then her grandfather wanted to put those fears to rest.

The sheriff's office approached Colon's attorney Murray with multiple offers to make the test more palatable for his client. Murray could have more control over the test and input in how the questions were framed, although the examiner would have final say on the questions. The FBI offered to fly in one of their top experts to administer the test. The final proposal was if the examiner concluded Colon had passed the polygraph, the district attorney would issue a statement that Colon was no longer a suspect. Even with the concessions of law enforcement, Colon still refused. He continued to deny to local reporters that he could have harmed Samantha and claimed to have had no involvement in her disappearance.

A small group of volunteers kept looking for any sign of Samantha despite the weather. Temperatures were in the 20s, and the daily snow flurries didn't let up. The promise of high-tech equipment from the FBI brought a full suspension of the search, however. Fingers were crossed that the additional equipment would bring resolution and locate Samantha.

While search volunteers went home, the wintry weather only added to our caseload. The evening of March 6 brought more motor vehicle accidents because of the treacherous road conditions. The dispatcher sent the call for assistance at the railroad crossing on Miller Road outside of Warsaw around 9:30 PM. A man had lost control of his pickup as he approached the tracks, and the truck slid through the crossing, becoming jammed on the rails. A Canadian-Pacific train was bearing down on the truck, and the driver finally abandoned the vehicle, which saved his life. Fortunately, no one was injured; the engine sustained only minor damage, but the truck was totaled. The 1994 Chevy had been carried three-tenths of a mile down the tracks before the train had been able to stop. Railroad officials were called to come and inspect the tracks as we talked with the driver and the train crew. A tow truck was on its way to extract the truck when a call came across the radio about a suicidal man who was also threatening a woman with a rifle in the Township of Gainesville. Then another call crackled across our radios with a report of a DWI accident in Bennington. The driver had lost control of his van on Route 354, skidding off the shoulder and plunging down an embankment into a tree. The stack of case files rose higher on everyone's desks.

CHAPTER 9

Friday, March 7, 1997

I was making a series of phone calls Friday morning to try and find Samantha's blood type. My first call was to the Florida hospital where she was born. After talking with the records department, I discovered that it was standard procedure for umbilical cord blood to be taken at birth. This was good news, I thought. The blood type would then be documented on the infant's birth records. The information was normally kept for five years and then destroyed. Disappointment came when they told me that Samantha's blood type hadn't been recorded on any remaining records the Jackson Memorial Hospital in Miami had on file. We also knew she'd been seen by a doctor in 1994, but the call to the doctor's office in Florida turned up nothing. The Letchworth School District had no record of her blood type either. I was frustrated with the lack of any help from medical records, and nothing had been collected from her home that we absolutely knew was her blood. We desperately needed a sample that would help identify the blood evidence sitting in the crime lab.

Investigator Dennis Spink, Special Agents Ken Eggleston, and Mike Liwicki were back in the field, interviewing more people who'd had contact with Stra and Colon. One neighbor who knew Lisa Johnson called her on February 27 to see if she could help the family in any way. The press, law enforcement, and the search were overwhelming for everyone. The neighbor couldn't imagine the grief over a missing child.

Lisa asked if she could babysit Angela and Cassandra, which surprised her. The neighbor agreed even though she didn't know the children, but she wanted to help out in this crisis. Lisa dropped off the girls around 5:00 PM and fully expected Rachel or Angel to pick them up that evening, but no one came to the neighbor's door. She finally put them to bed and slept on the couch in case Rachel came during the night for them. No one came for them Friday morning either, and it wasn't until 7:30 PM that night Bruno knocked at the door to tell her that Rachel and Angel should be by soon to pick up the girls. In fact, Bruno returned at 9:30 PM and took his granddaughters with him. The neighbor told investigators that the girls were very quiet and didn't ask for their parents. Angela watched a TV news report about Samantha's disappearance while eating lunch that day, but made no comment on it. The woman and her husband had found the experience with the emotionless little girls unsettling.

The director of The Learning Center in Perry, NY told the FBI about the sign-in time for the sisters the day of Samantha's disappearance. She also related the conversation she'd had with Colon at 4:35 PM on Thursday. He called to say that the sheriff's office was on the way and they had a "situation." When he found out that there was an additional charge for every 15 minutes after 5:30 PM, he assured the director, Tamra O'Connor, he would be there as soon as possible. He beat the deadline and picked up the girls at 5:20 PM. There were no startling leads or new information that would help move the investigation in the right direction.

Another examination of the Bronco fell to me that afternoon, and I had the SUV (garaged at Ott's Collision Service in South Warsaw) carried by flatbed to the county highway department's mechanical garage. Crawling underneath the vehicle, I was able to collect soil samples from the undercarriage. We checked the heater coil to see if a possible antifreeze leak might be the reason for the saturated carpet. A small leak was discovered, and it could at least partially account for the wet carpet on the passenger side. After the examination of the Bronco, it was transported back to the Sheriff's Office.

In the early evening, a call came in from a tipster that was chilling. The caller asked if the water tower in Perry had been checked. The person was concerned about the similarities in the current case with the Kali Ann Poulton kidnapping and murder that had taken place in Rochester, NY in 1994. Only now was the killer, Mark Christie, headed for trial after an exhaustive and persistent investigation by the Monroe County Sheriff's Office. Kali Ann's body had been found in a 30,000-gallon water tank next to the murderer's workplace. Champion Products in Perry, Angel's former employer, was near the same type of water tank. It needed to be checked out, the caller insisted. I agreed.

Saturday, March 8, 1997

The investigation into Samantha Zaldivar's disappearance was now eleven days old. Mounting frustration over the lack of any real progress was taking its toll on everyone. We were looking hard at Colon, but we had no concrete evidence linking him to the disappearance. There was no sign of Samantha found during the search. We were waiting for blood test results and other forensic tests to be completed. The community was understandably impatient for answers. It was a case everyone took personally.

Angel Colon and his attorney repeatedly told the media that Colon was the prime suspect. Undersheriff Ely denied their assertion but also said if the pair believed Angel was the top suspect, then there must be a reason for them to say that. No arrangements were made for the polygraph despite further negotiations. Colon was also experiencing the community's anger. Many were pointing the finger at him and

Rachel. The messy family situation was all over the news, keeping pressure on the couple.

Ely went public with a request for witnesses that may have seen the 1988 Bronco leave the trailer park between the hours of midnight and 5:00 AM on February 26. We had the neighbor's statement, but additional corroboration would greatly help, especially if we could discover where the vehicle had gone. Its final destination was still a mystery, and the soil samples and other evidence from the vehicle had failed to solve it.

I met with the undersheriff, Investigators Davis, Eck, Donnelly, and Spink, along with Captain John Copeland and Sheriff Capwell on that Saturday, March 8. We worked on ground and air maps for further searches, confirming latitude and longitude coordinates for each area. The group also discussed the water tower issue, and we agreed it needed to be checked out.

Investigator David Davis made arrangements with Champion Products maintenance supervisor Gary Beagle to look at the possibility of access to the water tower. The pair combed the property around the water tower, looking for any sign of entry into the tower area, but found none. The seasoned investigator determined that there was no sign of illegal entry to the tower. However, a large dumpster caught his attention, and he made a few calls to find out about the garbage company's pick-up schedule. He learned that the dumpster was emptied on Monday, Wednesday, and Friday mornings. I tried calling CID, the disposal company, but the office in Chaffee, NY was closed, and we had no emergency contact numbers. Finally, late on Sunday, March 9, Undersheriff Ely was able to talk with Michael Glasner, an employee of CID. After being told that it was possible a body had been put in the dumpster, Glasner agreed to meet me first thing on Monday morning at the Chaffee landfill to talk about our next move. The reality that we were looking to recover Samantha's body was difficult to process. We had maintained high hopes of finding her alive. To think she might be discarded in a garbage dump was more than disturbing.

CHAPTER 10

Monday, March 10, 1997

I arrived before 8:00 AM to talk with Michael Glasner, who was waiting for me at the CID landfill on NYS Route 16. Looking out over the vast landfill, it became mind-boggling to even know where we would begin to try and locate a little girl's body. I soon learned that the waste disposal business is much more organized and detailed than I imagined.

Glasner offered his full cooperation with the investigation and was working to contact the company president. He had already talked with the operator of the loader who handled the contents of the dumpsters transported from Champion. The man had remembered the load coming from Perry on February 26. I needed to talk to him and went out to locate Robert Ressler.

Once I began interviewing him, I formed a slim hope we were on the right track. The load on February 26 had stuck in his mind because the usual trash was cloth and cardboard in clear plastic bags. But a dark-colored bag that appeared to be quite heavy had dropped out of the load that day, which was unusual. He expected lighter garbage—the bags normally rolled onto the ground, but the one garbage bag didn't. The contents of the bag were unknown. As much as this sounded like a possible lead, the bad news followed quickly behind it. Eight hundred tons of garbage was dumped each day in the area. It would be a Herculean task to even make a dent in searching for one garbage bag that was now buried in tons of trash.

Once CID was aware of the predicament, they made arrangements for loads coming in that day to be disposed of in another section, to avoid compounding the problem. However, there was another issue, and that was financial. It would be an expensive endeavor to hunt through the refuse of the last week-and-a-half. CID also had to contact the NYS Department of Environmental Conservation (DEC) for permission to dig out and search the identified zone. There were also costs involved that the county would have to approve. CID had to charge us for assisting in the search, which would be $720 a day. A four-day search would cost $2,880. The company would make every effort to trim the expense as much as they could. The president hoped he could reduce the cost by 25 to 50 percent. The time and resources invested in the case were already taking a bite out of the sheriff's annual budget, and this additional expense might be denied. I called Allen Capwell with the information.

Sheriff Capwell and Undersheriff Ely reached out immediately to the Chairman of the Board of Supervisors, Tom Moran. Tom had long been a supporter of law enforcement and threw his full backing behind the effort. He went to bat for the landfill search with the rest of the board, and it came through. With the money hurdle out of the way, I waited to hear from CID. The call came later in the afternoon, which was good news. The DEC had approved the request. Deputies Edward Till and Daniel Hummel were assigned with me to assist with the landfill excavation. We had no idea what we would find over the next three days, the designated time for the search.

Samantha's family was constantly inundated with reporters, who were trying to uncover anything new in the case. Many times Rachel and Angel sought refuge across the street with Lisa and Bruno. Lisa had instructions from the undersheriff to call if the media's persistent presence became too much. Lisa made a few calls for assistance, and a deputy was assigned to block off her driveway with his car, effectively keeping the press from gaining access to her home. Others were also interested in the disappearance and the notoriety surrounding the case. Bruno Stra had been contacted by the psychic Sylvia Browne, who offered help. The family was grasping for anything or anyone who could help find Samantha. Browne was a regular on the *Montel Williams* and *Larry King* talk shows and was debunked consistently in her predictions of the whereabouts of missing persons. Her meager success rate, however, brought them a ray of hope, and Bruno took the list of impressions from the self-proclaimed clairvoyant. No one knows how much information she gleaned from the family and newspaper articles before making her predictions. There were already plenty of theories offered by community members about Angel Colon's involvement, as well as finger-pointing at Rachel. The search had also retained a tight perimeter, with the trailer in the center. Browne's suggestions that the little girl "wasn't far from home" and that abuse was involved were already on everyone's minds. We were about to find out if Samantha had been taken farther from home.

Tuesday, March 11, 1997

Chaffee, NY is a hamlet located in the southeast portion of Erie County. New York State Route 16, where the landfill is located, is a heavily-trafficked truck route to the southern tier of the state. Garbage from all over Wyoming County and several other counties was hauled in each day. The landfill itself took up fifty-one acres.

An artic wind hit our faces when we left our vehicles in the driveway and walked out to meet the waiting officials. Once again, winter weather was a factor, and temperatures were only in the 20s. We were told that the section to be examined was 100 feet by 150 feet and 28 feet deep. Deputies Till and Hummel and I all looked at each other, feeling stunned at the work ahead. Hummel shook his head and murmured, "You've gotta be kidding."

Dirt roads crisscrossed the immense area, and we drove our cars quite a way from the office to the search area. It was at the top of a hill, leaving us more exposed to the wind. The area was marked off and flagged to keep us in the correct section, and we systematically worked backward. We were not only looking for Samantha's body, but also for pieces of clothing or the *Aladdin* backpack she was supposed to be wearing when she'd left for the bus that February morning. As the hours wore on that first day, we realized that the three of us hadn't considered the weather conditions and the exposed area where we would be working. Fingers and toes were numb as we combed through the front loader's bucket, looking for a purple jacket or a backpack or Samantha. Opening garbage bags, we dumped out countless piles of disgusting refuse to ensure nothing was missed. The stench was incredible.

We dressed in much warmer clothes the next two days, continuing to dig through mounds of unimaginable trash for ten hours or more each day. Once in a while, we would spot a backpack and extract it carefully. Every time one was located, everyone stopped in silence while it was examined. Disappointment followed every time. Not one *Aladdin* backpack was unearthed. No purple jacket was sighted—no body. We gained a great appreciation for the way the garbage was dumped in the landfill and the recordkeeping that identified the area we needed to investigate. We also learned a lot about people's lives in sorting through so much waste. Just about anything you can imagine ends up in the landfill. It would have been all right with me not to have seen some of it.

At the end of the third day, we reached the culmination of the concentrated search. There was nothing. Not one single thing that would lead us to believe Samantha had been tossed in the dumpster in Perry. I always went into investigations with high hopes of catching a break. When we came up empty-handed once again, it seemed that we were on an emotional roller-coaster, one that had to be much worse for Samantha's family. It was exacting a toll on Bruno, who had been taken once already to the hospital to be checked out.

While I was searching the Chaffee landfill, the FBI had brought in high-tech equipment to aid in the search around the trailer park and surrounding area. The exact type of equipment was kept from the press at the time. Undersheriff Ely had declined to tip law enforcement's hand publicly about the specialized tools used to locate Samantha.

Rachel and her attorney were in Family Court and agreed to allow blood samples to be taken from Angela and Cassandra that day. The girls were brought to the Wyoming County Community Hospital and the samples were drawn. Investigator Eck returned with the blood samples, which I would soon take to the crime lab.

Wednesday, March 12, 1997

The FBI's command center in the county's Public Safety building was humming with constant activity. Angel Colon's photo was alongside Samantha's. A timeline was tacked on the wall as well, along with posters listing the details of the investigation—down to what movies Angel had watched prior to Samantha's disappearance and the time the neighbor heard a vehicle leave the trailer park. The sheriff had gotten permission from the board of supervisors to purchase computers in order to use case management software from the FBI. The department was behind in the technology game at that time. We didn't even have a laptop, but we were quickly gaining ground due to the demands of the case.

We needed to coordinate the information we did have and peel back the layers of the story. More people came forward with bits of information about Angel. We didn't know if they were significant, but we weren't about to take any chances, so we continued to take statements.

It appeared Angel had made an effort to convince former coworkers and neighbors of his innocence since WCDSS had removed his daughters. He reeled off stories of his commitment to his family and how much he loved Samantha. He felt discriminated against because he was "Spanish." One acquaintance believed he was working on her sympathies so she would offer him a place to stay. Everyone knew the situation he was in. He'd been ordered to vacate the residence in order for Rachel to have Angela and Cassandra returned home. He'd struck out in finding a place to live in Wyoming County, and Rachel's attorney Anthony Irrera reported that he was now in Valdosta, Georgia. But the DSS was unable to verify an address and refused to return the girls without proof of his relocation. There was more cause for concern because of conversations the girls had had in the temporary foster home. Their comments led us to believe Colon was habitually abusing Samantha. One of the girls had said, "Poppy hits Takita all the time." Poppy was what they called Angel, and Takita was Samantha's nickname.

Rachel was threatening to stop cooperating with authorities on the advice of her lawyer. The tangle of the family court process and the constant presence of the media had seemingly overwhelmed her. The WCDSS was ready to file a violation petition against Colon because he had left the area without informing them of his new address. Rachel and her attorney insisted that he was living with his mother and sister in Georgia. She had been granted a supervised visit with the girls the day before, which according to her and

Irerra had gone well. She told reporters she was heartbroken leaving her daughters. She was alone at the trailer—one daughter missing, two in foster care, Angel was long gone, and she had no transportation. She looked to the media and began enlisting more attention in the search for Samantha. She contacted the National Center for Missing and Exploited Children and the TV show *America's Most Wanted.*

We reached another dead end, two weeks after the initial report of Samantha's disappearance. The sophisticated equipment brought in by the FBI had failed to reveal anything that indicated where Samantha might be. We needed a real break.

CHAPTER 11

Thursday, March 13, 1997

In the late afternoon, Investigator Paul Donnelly had been working to follow up on telephone leads when he received another. A disturbing telephone call came in from the Cheektowaga Police Department, a suburb of Buffalo. A man who'd been listening to his CB radio heard an unnerving conversation between two truck drivers. Realizing it could be about Samantha, he'd gone to the police station to make a report. The two over-the-road drivers had been talking about looking for "young meat," 12-year-olds and younger. One driver mentioned he'd heard that another driver who was known to them had picked up a "seven-year-old girl" and had her at his trailer. Then directions were given to a trailer park south of Dayton, Ohio. The tipster had even heard the men discuss whether it was the girl that was missing in New York. One said, "Yeah, I think so." The investigator had another story to check out, which would eventually lead nowhere. We were spinning our wheels, which made everyone more determined to find out what had really happened to her. The expectation for a good outcome to the case had evaporated over the last two weeks.

Undersheriff Ely was angered to learn from a Buffalo, NY radio station that Angel Colon was now working on a fishing boat in the Florida Keys. Murray, Colon's attorney, had assured the sheriff's department he was in Georgia with family. Ely also had heard from Rachel and her attorney

Irerra that they would not cooperate any further with law enforcement until the girls were returned home. There would be no progress for anyone, especially Rachel. This meant more delays in having Angela and Cassandra returned to her. With Angel's true address still in question, the DSS wasn't going to allow her to regain custody, and with allegations of possible child abuse, the girls would be examined before they would leave foster care. Rachel continued to support Colon, refusing to believe any allegation that connected him to Samantha's disappearance or that he had harmed his biological children. It seemed outrageous to many, including me. He was the person of interest, and we weren't even sure where he really was. We still didn't have enough to arrest him.

Another house fire, this time on Blackhouse Road in the Town of Middlebury, drew our attention momentarily away from the complexities of the Zaldivar investigation. I was grateful there were no injuries, but the house was a total loss due to an electrical issue with a dryer. At least we had answers for the owners about the reasons for the fire. And then a call came in reporting an armed robbery of a video rental store in Silver Springs. It was similar to an armed robbery just days before in the Village of Warsaw. Fortunately, the clerks in both stores weren't injured, and the robber had taken the cash from the registers and run. Investigator Donnelly added this case to the pile he was working on. We wanted to catch the perpetrator before someone got hurt or worse.

By this time, rumors of all sorts were circulating through the Letchworth School District communities. School administration had real concerns for their students, especially those who were Samantha's classmates in Primary House, which was a large class of at least forty, and those who rode her bus, who numbered another fifty. School district superintendent Joseph Backer put in place a crisis team to provide counseling for students. The county's Office of Mental Health arranged for focus groups to allow students to talk about their fears and concerns. These groups were also forums to disseminate accurate information and put rumors to rest. Letters went out to parents with advice on handling their children's concerns without dismissing them. Teachers and counselors had daily challenges to help these young children work through their very real fears. Could they be taken by someone? Why would someone take Samantha? Where was she?

The crime lab sent out a report on the items we had taken from the trailer and Bronco in February. The stained blanket, a towel, hair, trash inside the vehicle, gloves, socks—several dozen items had gone to the lab for analysis. Without a suspect item to compare these with, it was a futile first round for definitive results. No seminal fluid had been found, but human blood had. Further testing was needed, and DNA was crucial to establish what had happened to Samantha.

Freezing rain continued to be a weather issue and caused dozens of motor vehicle accidents. Many Wyoming County schools had delayed opening by two hours. Accident reports took up much of the day for deputies.

Friday, March 14, 1997

Around 2:00 PM, I received instructions from Undersheriff Ely to return Colon's driver's license to his attorney. But the license wasn't in the evidence room; it had been delivered to the crime lab in Rochester. An envelope of documents found in the Bronco's glove compartment had become evidence when we'd processed the vehicle at the beginning of our investigation. An interim New York driver's license, a road test document, and registration DMV papers were waiting for further analysis because three pieces of the paper found in the envelope had red-brown stains, which appeared to be blood. In fact, the lab confirmed the presence of human blood on them. An inventory of the specific documents taken from the vehicle had yet to be given to Murray, Colon's attorney. Murray couldn't understand why the interim driver's license hadn't been returned to Colon in the first place, and we weren't ready to tell him the reason. Fortunately, the license was the one paper that didn't have any blood traces, so it could be returned. Jerry Stout got involved to smooth things over with the defense attorney, who was in and out of court hearings most of the day. Murray wasn't happy with the delay, although there were some other documents taken from Colon, including a copy of his birth certificate and some NYS benefit cards, which were returned to him that day. Over the course of the afternoon, a plan was made for me to retrieve his license on Monday, March 17 and hand it over to Murray then.

After almost ten days of being away from home, Angela and Cassandra were returned to their mother. Attorney Irrera and the WCDSS hammered out a solution. Judge Michael Griffith handed down the family court order with stiff conditions. Rachel couldn't travel out of state, and she would be closely supervised by Social Services. The most important stipulation by the judge was for Stra to end all contact with Angel Colon.

Although she was overjoyed to have her two daughters back home, she complained about the restrictions. She was unhappy about the rules that other parents didn't have to deal with.

Scott DeSmit, a reporter for *The Daily News* in Batavia, took up Stra's cause, urging readers to stop judging her for not being emotional enough, for supporting Colon, and being a neglectful mother. She told DeSmit that she believed Samantha had been abducted by someone in the driveway of the trailer park on her way to the bus. She absolutely stood by Colon's account of what had happened the morning of February 26. Not many people were buying her story though, and she felt the disapproval and suspicions of the community. Colon was reported to be in Marathon, Florida, safely out of the limelight in Hermitage. Colon's behavior the first night of the investigation, the observations of neighbors, the evidence taken from the trailer and Bronco, and Colon's CSVA results gave every indication that he knew what had happened to Samantha.

But without evidence that could stand up in court and with Samantha still missing, we were stonewalled. One crucial element we needed was a sample of her blood to extract DNA. Until we found Samantha or the right piece of evidence that unequivocally connected Colon to her disappearance, we had to keep working.

Exhaustion was overtaking everyone in the sheriff's department. Road patrols were doing much of the day-to-day work that usually went to investigators. Deputies were working extra shifts to maintain coverage throughout the county. Two-man cars were assigned to keep everyone alert throughout every shift. Investigators worked shoulder to shoulder with the FBI agents, following up leads and interviewing and re-interviewing all who knew Colon, Stra, and Samantha. It was difficult to deal with the lack of progress, but we dug in our heels to find this little girl, who should have been playing with her sisters and going to school.

Saturday, March 15, 1997

Another phone tip from a local resident led me to a field on the Shearing Farm, located on Fuller Road in the Town of Gainesville. The caller had talked to Undersheriff Ely, telling him that she felt that Samantha might be found in this muddy and snow-covered field. The undersheriff believed her suspicion should be checked out. Even if the "lead" seemed far-fetched, we took each one seriously. I gathered a soil sample from the area. It would be compared with the soil we'd taken from the undercarriage of the Bronco.

That night, TV's popular *America's Most Wanted* show featured Samantha's disappearance. We were flooded with even more tips after the show. They needed our attention but didn't bring us any closer to finding Samantha.

Monday, March 17, 1997

Another road trip to Rochester started my day as I delivered the soil sample for testing from the Shearing Farm and picked up Colon's interim license, which was Lab Label #14805, marked as #19 in our evidence log.

The reality is the majority of crime labs have a serious backlog of four or usually six and more weeks. Literally hundreds of cases were ahead of ours, although the director had made exceptions and accommodated special requests regarding the Zaldivar case. Many times evidence isn't analyzed until a trial is calendared. And then, decisions have to be made about which items of evidence will be examined. Which are most important? Which clearly show the perpetrator's guilt? We had already transported more than fifty pieces of evidence from the trailer and Bronco alone, which wasn't an unusual number for a lot of criminal cases. Law enforcement and the attorneys had to pick and choose their battles when it came to evidence analysis. We knew it was nearly impossible for all of the substances and objects to be tested.

After finishing at the lab, I drove to Batavia to deliver Colon's interim license to his attorney. Murray was out of the office, and I finally gave the paper to his secretary and requested a receipt.

The National Center for Missing and Exploited Children in Rochester began its campaign to find Samantha. Rachel and her attorney attended a news conference in Rochester to support the organization's huge effort to locate her daughter. Thousands of posters were printed, which were widely distributed to the public and law enforcement. The internet and fax machines would be used to disseminate the information worldwide. With more publicity, maybe someone would come forward with what we needed to know.

Colon's court date in the Town of Wethersfield was scheduled for the evening, but the town justice adjourned his appearance until April 22. His attorney had requested a forty-five-day adjournment in order to file motions. There was plenty of skepticism about him ever appearing. Why should he come back? A misdemeanor charge was nothing. Why would we pursue him out of state?

CHAPTER 12

Tuesday, March 18, 1997

The cadaver dog handler, Bill Tolhurst of the Niagara County Sheriff's Office, handed over a scent pad to be kept in the evidence refrigerator. The scent pad was made of sterile gauze pads and had been placed on clothing belonging to Samantha. The pads retain the odor of the person and are placed with gloved hands in unused plastic bags, double sealed with packing tape. The pad would be available when the dogs were prepared for their next search in the area.

The dogs came up empty that day, just as we did. Investigators Spink and Eck had accompanied me with Tolhurst to search more fields around Fuller Road in the Town of Gainesville. We spent time looking in the woods and fields in the vicinity of Bugg Road in the Town of Wethersfield. No lead panned out that day for anyone.

However, the piece of foam from the mattress in Samantha's room and the cotton swabs used to dab the bedrail (which had tested positive for blood) were expedited by the Monroe County Crime Lab to the New York State Police Forensic Center in Albany. They would do the DNA testing. We had blood samples from Rachel, Noel, Angela, and Cassandra to compare to the Forensic Center's findings.

Spring break was starting, and my family vacation—which had been planned months prior—was about to begin. We headed out to Myrtle Beach, South Carolina. I was ready for some time away from the intensity of work, and my wife

Pam, who was a teacher at Lockwood Elementary, was too. While I was gone, the investigation continued without interruption with significant evidence being collected.

Friday, March 21, 1997

Rachel had finally come up with a hair sample of Samantha's. She agreed to give us a lock of baby hair that had been kept in a baby book. Investigator Gary Eck drove to the trailer to pick up the first tangible biological evidence we knew was from Samantha. However, it wouldn't provide DNA since it had been snipped from her head. Only hair follicles with a root that have been pulled from the body were a source of DNA—at least at that time. We also had permission to take hair samples from Rachel, Angela, and Cassandra for comparison. After collecting hair, Investigator Eck labeled each sample and secured them in the evidence room.

The FBI was right on his heels that day. They'd arranged to once again look for evidence in Stra's trailer. At the beginning of the investigation, we'd been looking for a missing child—possibly kidnapped. But early on, we were quite sure something terrible had happened to Samantha in her home. We had no hard proof. In the late afternoon, a team of agents along with Captain Michael Melton of the Amherst Police Department, who was a crime scene photographer, drove into the trailer park in Hermitage. They were looking specifically for blood evidence and would use luminol to attempt to identify any areas with blood residue.

Stra and her attorney Irrera met the team at the front door. Stra signed a "consent search" and led the men to a bathroom at the front of the mobile home, next to the girls' bedroom, while Investigator Spink was on standby outside the trailer.

Everyone is familiar with luminol and its connection to forensic science. TV portrays it as a magical substance that crime scene investigators spray on surfaces and immediately a blue glow jumps out to show them blood spray or bloody drag marks that the criminal has tried to remove. The reality is different and requires skill in the application of the chemical and long-exposure photography to determine if blood is present, along with follow-up testing in a lab.

Luminol is a white powder which, when diluted with an oxidizing agent, will react to several different substances. It not only reacts to blood, but to bleach, metals such as copper or iron, and specific plant materials. When luminol reacts with an oxidizing agent such as hydrogen peroxide and then meets a catalyst such as blood or bleach, chemiluminescence occurs, which is similar to the light from fireflies or glow sticks. In order to observe the blue glow, the room must be darkened. The reaction only lasts about thirty seconds. Reapplication of luminol is necessary to initiate another reaction. The crime scene photographer must set up a long-exposure photograph of several minutes to capture the blue glow.

Scientists began studying luminol in the late 1920s, and by the 1930s, it was used at crime scenes. A steady hand is required when spraying it over a surface. It must be applied evenly to produce effective results.

After mixing up a bottle of luminol, a penny was placed on the bathroom floor to use as a positive control for the test. A positive reaction was observed after luminol was sprayed on the penny. They were ready to go.

The team sprayed the liquid on the floor in front of the sink/vanity, which tested positive. Crime scene technicians took several long-exposure photographs of varying lengths and sprayed and photographed the vanity door. It looked like blood had covered every surface of the bathroom. After about ninety minutes of testing, it was terminated with inconclusive results. Once SA Crino learned that the mobile home park used a well as its water source, he knew he had false-positive results. Even though there were positive reactions, the iron content in the water would react to the luminol. Packing up their equipment with frustrated expressions on their faces, the agents and Captain Melton slipped on their coats and headed back to their vehicles.

The next stop for the team was the Wyoming County Sheriff's Department storage facility. A presumptive test for blood residue would be performed on Colon's SUV. The 1988 Ford was parked in a single garage there and would be examined again. This was a second attempt to find blood on the passenger seat. We believed at the onset that blood was present, but our initial testing had turned up nothing. The suspicious stain would be tested again with a different technique.

Sheriff's investigator Dave Davis joined the team and went to locate the key to the facility. He unlocked the garage around 7:15 PM. The team went to work and used Hemastix® test strips on the passenger's seat, which reacted instantly, indicating iron was present. Therefore, in all likelihood, it was blood. By holding filter paper, pressing harder against the soft seat surface where the stain was located, and waiting longer, a better sample was obtained. The team tested the driver's seat, which also reacted positively, although the reaction was delayed. The shift lever, turning signal lever, steering wheel, driver's side door handle, the backrest on the passenger's seat, passenger-side kick panel, and passenger-side seatbelt were negative for blood. The team immediately tagged the passenger seat as evidence. Everyone dated and signed their initials on the lower section of the seat. Was the blood human? The Hemastix® doesn't differentiate between human and animal blood. Was it Samantha's or someone else's blood?

Investigator Davis secured the vehicle and the seat in the garage, and the men called it a night.

Saturday, March 22, 1997

A call came from Bruno on Saturday morning. Around 10:00 AM, he'd been traveling on Shearing Road in the Town of Gainesville. Something white caught his eye in a swampy area off the road. Bruno stopped and worked his way into the boggy section and retrieved a white sheet. Noticing some unknown stains on it, he took it with him and wanted to turn it in as possible evidence.

The sheriff's department secured the sheet and successfully dried it out. Eventually the item was packaged properly, and when I returned from vacation, I transported it to the Monroe County Crime Lab for further analysis. The lab tested it and quickly determined there was no blood on the fabric. Once again, a tip that held the promise of good information evaporated. It seemed to be the norm in this case, but the daily tips that came in were all treated seriously. We knew from experience that even the smallest bit of evidence could be integral in finding out what had happened to Samantha.

CHAPTER 13

Thursday, April 3, 1997

With still no credible leads on the case, we continued multiple investigations that were pending throughout the end of March. Investigators also made time to follow up on any leads that came in from phone calls. Undersheriff Ely drove out to see Rachel after receiving a phone call from her. She had discovered one of Samantha's baby teeth and wanted to turn it over. The tooth could prove useful as teeth and bones are sources of DNA. The process of extracting it is not a speedy one, and we knew we would have to wait for answers from the lab.

The community and law enforcement were intent on another coordinated search for Samantha. Everyone had a singular goal in mind, and that was to find Samantha. Sheriff Capwell, Captain John Copeland, and Jack Fisher, the Wyoming County Fire Coordinator, headed up a group of volunteers and law enforcement officers. They began planning for the most complex and extensive search the county had ever undertaken. The search encompassed six towns with a total of twenty-two specific areas. This was in addition to other areas officers had been checking regularly since day one. Some of the previous search areas would be gone over again to make sure nothing had been missed. Since February, searches had been performed in ten different townships and in more than forty different areas.

The coordinators scheduled specific dates for the massive search effort by law enforcement and the community for the weekend of April 19 and April 20. Word was getting out about the plan, and people everywhere were offering to help. A variety of K-9 groups, mounted patrols, volunteer agencies, local schools, federal and state agencies, volunteer firemen, and military contacted the search coordinators and offered to help. Citizens throughout Wyoming County and all of New York State were ready to join the others. The outpouring of community support statewide was overwhelming. Those coordinating the search had a huge task to ensure that things like transportation, housing, food, training, and medical assistance were at the ready. Communications personnel were needed. The event was heavily publicized, and the parents of the murdered Kali Ann Poulton of Rochester, NY made plans to be part of the search effort.

In addition to the huge number committed to the search, there was another group who volunteered time and money to feed searchers. Some housed out-of-town volunteers, while others helped with transportation. A nearby fire hall opened up to house even more people. Without the generosity of donors, the search would have been cut back because of the astronomical cost. Businesses and individuals contributed heavily in both food and monetary donations. We even saw children breaking into their piggy banks to help. Grocery stores, local restaurants, individuals, and local volunteer fire departments donated 2,500 hotdogs, 2,500 hamburgers, meatballs, BBQ pork, rolls, donuts, cookies, and eggs, along with plates and plastic utensils, bottled water, coffee, garbage bags, and more. The outpouring of concern and generosity was staggering.

Saturday, April 19 and Sunday, April 20, 1997

As the long weeks of planning unfolded on a wintery Saturday, numerous staging areas were set up around the Hermitage area. Two medical staging areas, six ambulance stand-by areas, five different staging areas for volunteer coordination, an incident command post, an information officer post, and a food staging area were established. Radio operators were also critical for communication, and the team was ready. One medical assistance area was at the North Java Fire Hall on NYS Route 98, another at the Wethersfield Highway Department barns on NYS Route 78. Food was served at the Gainesville Fire Department. Groups of volunteers were coordinated at the old Ames store parking lot in Warsaw on NYS Route 19, North Java Fire Hall, Letchworth School, the County Highway Department on NYS Route 19, and the Wethersfield Town barns on NYS Route 78.

Wyoming County Coroner Mike Smith manned a table to screen volunteers at the Ames parking lot. He interviewed a steady stream of people, gathering basic information, and learned that many who lived outside Wyoming County were offering to help. As they formed groups, Mike gave them instructions about how to conduct themselves. They were to strictly follow the instructions of the group leader. Groups would form straight lines and stay together as they searched. No one was to go off on their own. If they did spot something, they were not to pick it up or even touch it. The appropriate people would be called to check it out. Mike was amazed at the number of people from Rochester and Buffalo who came in dress clothes and nice shoes, totally unprepared for the rigorous terrain in Hermitage. But all were willing to give up their time to look for Samantha. The coroner was also blown away by the community's support. Sandwiches showed up at the station brought in by local stores to help feed volunteers.

"Nobody asked, but suddenly it was there. Hearts opened up," he said.

The weather was against us again with cold temperatures, a sharp breeze, snow, mud, and standing water. It seemed the elements were determined to make the search more difficult. Everyone ready to go in Hermitage was bundled up in winter garb and sturdy boots. The search area was a designated five-mile radius around the trailer park, and searchers were sent out in small groups to slog through fields and woods. K-9 groups and searchers on horseback went into different locations to scour brush and creeks for any sign of Samantha. More than 1,700 searchers headed out from the staging areas during the weekend. Most of the men and women had never participated in a search effort, especially of this magnitude, and were quickly trained by group leaders before going out. Although conditions were less than ideal, no one complained.

Shoulder to shoulder, they trekked through fields, some with poles to poke through snow in hopes of finding Samantha. No one had any illusions—it was a recovery search. Group leaders commented that they had never headed up a more dedicated, hardworking, and energetic group of volunteers. A local resident I spoke with remarked she was proud to be a member of the community because the volunteers came together with one purpose—to find Samantha. But despite the massive effort of the community and outside agencies, the two-day search ended on a low note. No credible evidence had been collected, and Samantha had not been located. Even though many volunteers asked when the next search would be organized, we would not schedule another one. Discouragement was palpable for law enforcement. We were tired, physically and emotionally. The lack of any real progress was beyond frustrating.

Friday, April 25, 1997

After the letdown of the unsuccessful search, we received yet another phone call from a local resident. The man had found a large piece of what appeared to be skin on his property, and I went out to investigate. Once I took a look, I agreed that it was skin, but there was no way to tell if it was human or animal. After securing it in a metal can, I returned to the office to refrigerate the specimen in the evidence room. It was later transported to the crime lab to await analysis. It would be determined to be animal and not human.

Monday, April 28, 1997

The papers reported that Rachel was appearing on talk shows to spread the word of Samantha's disappearance. Rolanda Watts, a popular talk show host of the show *Rolanda*, featured the story in an episode entitled, "My Children Vanished without a Trace." It was also reported that both Stra and Colon would appear on the *Geraldo Rivera Show*, which was taped in New York City.

While there appeared to be a lull in the Zaldivar investigation, the investigative team had no downtime. Every spare minute was devoted to numerous other cases, but one that required significant attention was a horrific home invasion that had occurred in early January 1997. Investigator Spink and I were involved in the follow-up on the case. It had started as a home invasion and ended in rape and assault at a private residence in the Town of Eagle. The seventy-seven-year-old victim was raped, and her elderly husband was pistol-whipped. This case was a big deal, and investigators worked tirelessly for months. District Attorney Gerald Stout and Assistant District Attorney David DiMatteo worked side-by-side with investigators daily. When the Zaldivar case began in earnest for the DA's office, ADA

DiMatteo became the lone prosecutor as DA Stout took the lead in the Zaldivar case. Dennis Spink and I continued to work on this case along with DiMatteo for the next nine months until it was taken to the grand jury. Many Saturdays found the three of us working both the home invasion case and the Zaldivar case.

Days before the search, I had three high school students studying criminal justice at the Charles G. May Occupational Center in Mt. Morris shadow me for the day as part of the Boards of Cooperative Educational Services (BOCES) program. Commitments made months in advance had to be met, no matter how hectic the schedule. Just days after the search, it was "Take Your Daughter to Work" day, and my daughter joined me along with a morning group of eight students and sixteen students in the afternoon. In addition to Q-and-A sessions, the students received a tour of the sheriff's office. At the end of April, two Genesee Community College students from the criminal justice class spent the day with me. That same day, the NYS Police Forensic Center in Albany sent its report to the crime lab in Rochester.

Wednesday, April 30, 1997

The Forensic Center had completed analysis of several items for DNA, and the Assistant Director and Forensic Scientist sent their report to the director of the Monroe County Crime Lab. The bedrail with the bloodstain taken from the bedrail brought us no results. The blood was either too degraded or insufficient in size to produce any DNA findings. But despite those disappointing results, the small piece of foam produced a DNA sample.

The lab had the test tubes of blood from Noel Zaldivar, Rachel, Angela, and Cassandra to compare against the blood on the mattress foam. None of these individuals matched the DNA on the foam. The four could be excluded as having bled on the foam. However, the person who had bled on the foam couldn't be excluded as the offspring of Noel and Rachel.

CHAPTER 14

May 1 – May 20, 1997

The month of May sped by as we continued investigative work on dozens of outstanding cases. There was a good feeling when a file was ready to be closed. The largest file remained open with no credible leads or definitive evidence that would help us with the Zaldivar case.

We were constantly undermanned during the month, and I lent a hand in numerous transports from the jail to court to assist the road patrol, which was unable to cover everything that was going on. A large group of students from Warsaw Central School, grades five to eleven, visited the sheriff's office early in the month, and I enjoyed the more positive duty of talking with young people about the responsibilities of the job. They were eager to learn all they could about law enforcement and were full of questions. That was a bright spot for me. There was also an easy assignment on my way home one night. A motorist in the Village of Silver Springs needed help because he'd locked his keys in his car. It was good to quickly resolve that problem for him and go on home.

Wednesday, May 21, 1997

The day began with a meeting at the sheriff's office that included FBI special agents, Undersheriff Ely, Director Rodwell, Investigators Spink and Eck, and me. We discussed the various pieces of evidence we had and how we should proceed. The conversation was bleak—we discussed whether or not Samantha would ever be located and whether we would be able to make an arrest. There were still many pieces of the puzzle left to find, but as we sat around the table, there was a commitment to persevere and solve the case. We didn't realize that day how close we really were.

Friday, May 23, 1997

A follow-up meeting at the Rochester crime lab took place in the morning. We discussed the evidence that had been collected and what might be sent to the Forensic Center in Albany. After leaving the lab, I was looking forward to watching my son pitch for the Castile Little League team that evening. The game was at 6:00 PM in the Town of Wethersfield, and I was anticipating a night off and a chance to spend time with my family.

I was off-duty when a phone call was made at 4:21 PM to the sheriff's office from a woman at Rowe's General Store in Hermitage. She reported that Frank Conrad, an elderly farmer who was plowing a field in the Town of Wethersfield, had found a body. He was terribly shaken by the grisly discovery, and Deputy Miller was the first on the scene and went up to the field to see for himself. There was no question there was a body, and he called on Investigator Davis, who immediately drove out to meet with him and take Conrad's statement.

Undersheriff Ely was right behind Davis. At 4:25 PM, I received a call that a body had been discovered off Shaw Road in the Town of Wethersfield. Shaw Road was where the ball diamond was located and where I intended to be a spectator in the stands, watching my son play ball. I quickly headed out to the site to meet with Undersheriff Ely. When I arrived, Ron immediately told me that a portion of an arm and small hand were visible above the dirt. They could see a bit of a purple jacket as well. My heart sank. I knew we were about to find the most important piece of the puzzle. It wasn't the outcome I had hoped for over the weeks since the end of February. It was time to find out what had happened to Samantha.

Investigator Davis shared what he had learned from the farmer. He had decided to plow the long-fallow field that day. It hadn't been plowed in several years and should have been plowed weeks before, but on the spur-of-the-moment, Mr. Conrad had decided to finish his workday in that field. He was using a disc plow behind the tractor and had just started his second pass through the field when he thought he'd spotted an object on the edge of the field. He continued plowing and made several other passes until the wind caught his hat and blew it to the area where he'd glimpsed a bit of purple color above the soil. Driving the tractor toward his hat, he climbed down and walked over to pick it up. He examined the area where he'd seen the purple object. Bending over, he decided to tug at the fabric to see what it was. It didn't budge, but a child's hand suddenly protruded from the ground. Gasping at the gruesome find, he turned and ran to the tractor, driving to the edge of the woods that lined the field. He hiked directly to Kersch's Lime Service in Hermitage, where he found a man and woman to tell about what lay up in his field. While the man stayed with the shaken farmer, the woman ran to call the sheriff's office.

A neighbor of Frank Conrad took me back to the scene where Deputy Steven Miller had already taped off the area and was protecting it until a full evidence team could arrive. I took a few preliminary photos and returned to my vehicle to await the others. We needed to have the right personnel ready to exhume the body and collect all the evidence. It would take many hands to complete it correctly. The FBI Evidence Response Team was enroute. Tim Crino had gotten the call at the Buffalo FBI office and wasted no time contacting the team.

I made a call to one of the coaches and advised him of the situation as the road to the ball diamond would be closed now because of the discovery. Soon the area would be swarming with law enforcement, and the respective coaches decided to postpone the game to another day. Normally the vehicles would have been arriving at the ball diamond across the road from the crime scene, and players would be warming up for the game scheduled at 6:00 PM. We didn't need curiosity seekers lurking, trying to catch a glimpse of what was happening in the field.

Then a NYS Police helicopter whirred toward the ball diamond and landed on the pitcher's mound. The grass flattened around its radius. The blades slowed, as the chopper sat waiting for me to climb in. Ironically, it landed at the game's scheduled time. Investigator Robert Bachorski of the NYS Police and I quickly determined our plan of action. Aerial photographs were needed of the field and burial site. Within minutes, we were hovering over the site, snapping pictures from every angle. The fluttering yellow crime scene ribbon marked off the grave in the freshly plowed field. About twenty minutes later, we were back on the ground.

When I returned to the scene, Undersheriff Ely informed me that we were still waiting for the FBI to arrive. A call then went to the Monroe County Medical Examiner's Office, and they advised us that they were on their way as well. More officers were now on the scene, and Investigator Davis kept a log of the arrival times of all who came to scene.

The coroner, Mike Smith, was in the middle of dinner at a restaurant with his wife to celebrate their anniversary, which had been the day before. His pager went off, and when he called the number, the sheriff told him about the situation. Assuring Sheriff Capwell he'd be there as soon as possible, he drove to the scene in his suit and dress shoes, anticipating he'd be on the sidelines. He quickly realized that he needed a change of clothes as temperatures dropped and the sun began to set. Finding his fireman's gear in his vehicle, he prepared for the work ahead of him.

Sheriff Capwell was there, nursing a puncture wound to his hand. He'd received the call about Mr. Conrad's find just as he'd been opening a can of deck stain to finish a home project. The screwdriver had slipped, injuring his hand, but he didn't have time to deal with the cut. He was needed at the scene. His memories of the night are still fresh.

"I was impressed with Steve and the people from the Monroe County Crime Lab in the way they went to recover the body. They made sure they didn't destroy anything. It took some time."

In fact, it took a lot of time. The next few hours proved to be hectic with multiple notifications to the Sheriff's Investigative Team, FBI, New York State Police, District Attorney Gerald Stout, and many others. The district attorney got the call on the golf course and came straight to Hermitage. While we waited for the medical examiner's personnel, the wood line area near the gravesite was examined and photographed. The area had been extensively searched in the beginning and many times after that. Even cadaver dogs had been used here without them alerting. This portion of the field was protected by trees, and snowpack was present there until April. We once again went over every inch and discovered a small area where someone had attempted to dig a hole that was several inches in depth. Because large trees sheltered the area, it would have been frozen hard and very difficult to dig by hand. It was easy to see why it had been abandoned, and the actual grave was in the dead-furrow of the field where it would have been easier to dig.

At 9:10 PM, the investigators from the medical examiner's office arrived. We met briefly to formulate a plan to complete the awful task before us. After eighty-seven days of searching for Samantha, we believed we'd found her only a little over a thousand feet from her home. At 9:20 PM, we began processing the gravesite, spreading plastic tarps and setting up portable lights. A patrol car's headlights also shone on the area. The media was camped out across the road with their cameras and lights trained on the gravesite. The sheriff had us point some of the lights back at them to protect the privacy of the victim and our investigation.

This type of crime scene was a first for me. Although I'd attended several seminars about this sort of evidence recovery, it's totally different when it's real. It was also one of those tasks you hope to never do. I wasn't lucky enough, I guess.

But we were fortunate for the help of multiple agencies that night. FBI agent Crino was an invaluable resource as he assisted and guided us through each step. I had brought brand new garden tools and sterilized the trowels, shovels, and metal rakes before using them. We had several different sizes of brand new paintbrushes for brushing soil off the body. Constant photographs were taken as we removed soil. Before-and-after photos were necessary as each layer was removed. After approximately an inch of soil had been removed within the perimeter, we sifted it through wooden-framed screens. Any pertinent evidence would be caught on the top of the screen. Investigators knelt on the ground to examine any bits left behind to determine if they had evidentiary value. Sifted soil was placed on tarps away from the gravesite to keep it separate from earth to be sifted. The process was much like an archeological dig. Each layer had to be taken off with extreme care.

At times I joined the FBI agents in hand-sifting the dirt, looking for anything unusual. We had only one opportunity to examine the soil and surrounding area to make sure nothing was missed. It was meticulous work, and we were committed to doing it right so as to not overlook any miniscule piece of evidence.

Conversation stopped, and silence fell on the entire team while we focused on every scoop of dirt. The realization that this was Samantha was hitting us all hard. We collected soil samples along with tree and plant roots that had cut marks on them. A dental stone cast was made of a shovel mark for future possible comparisons.

Now that enough soil had been removed from around the body, we could see it was indeed a small girl, buried facedown about a foot to eighteen inches in the ground. Her clothing was exactly as Angel Colon had described to us—the outfit she was supposed to be wearing when he said she went to board the school bus. "Angel" was printed in marker on the label of her jacket. However, there was no backpack that she would have had if she'd been on her way to school. That backpack was never found.

The coroner pronounced her dead, which allowed us to go forward with the removal. The coroner, who isn't required to be a medical doctor, acts as an investigator and an advocate for the deceased. Mike had been doing the job since 1985. He was also the assistant fire chief in Wyoming at that time and had been an EMT for many years. He'd been drawn to the coroner position because of a tragedy he witnessed in the 70s, when a friend had died in an auto accident. The parents had waited for the coroner for more than three hours while their deceased son lay in his wrecked vehicle. No one could move the body until the coroner had pronounced him. Mike decided that wouldn't happen with him if he ever got the job. He was true to his word.

In the course of my career in law enforcement, I witnessed more than 450 autopsies, but this body recovery would stand out as the worst for me. All of us were overcome with emotion as the laborious process stretched into the night, and there were no words to describe the tragic ending we were witnessing under the harsh work lights. Many of us had tear-filled eyes, and someone began to pray for Samantha when we were ready to remove her from the cold ground.

We placed paper bags over her hands and feet to preserve any evidence on them. Ever so carefully—Mike Smith along with John Cody and Dan Stifter of the medical examiner's office—picked her up and gently placed the body in the bag and then she was taken to the medical examiner's vehicle. I cleared the gravesite at 12:30 AM, May 24. Soil and root samples were secured in my vehicle, along with hair samples in evidence bags, and I placed them in the evidence room in the sheriff's office at 1:10 AM.

Reflecting on the day's events, I realized that many details had come together in order for us to find Samantha. The cold weather that had plagued us throughout the investigation and hampered the searches had forensically preserved Samantha's body. Frank Conrad lost his hat to a gust of wind, and it landed near the grave. The large disc plow he used ran over the location near the body and never altered the scene. It was by the grace of God he was able to locate the body and not damage the scene at all. The body was unearthed by the turn of the plow just enough to expose it. It was like it was meant to be.

CHAPTER 15

Saturday, May 24, 1997

Without much sleep if any at all, I drove into the parking lot of the Monroe County Medical Examiner's Office at 7:35 AM. My job was to photograph Samantha's clothing that had been removed from her body and the remains before and throughout the autopsy. I walked down the hallway with Dr. Thomas Smith, who would conduct the autopsy, and three staff members. Coroner Mike Smith was also present.

The cool, stainless steel environment of the room seemed eerie as the doctor prepared to begin his work, and I began my solemn task at 9:30 AM. It wasn't until 1:00 PM that I had taken the last photo. Dr. Smith completed the autopsy at 1:30 PM. Dental records had been compared, and x-rays, hair samples, blood typing, swabs of orifices, stomach contents, and tissue samples had all been completed. We had high hopes that Samantha's body would yield the evidence we needed.

Dr. Smith's preliminary findings were as we feared. Although there was much more work to do, the ugly truth of what had happened to the seven-year-old was now in an official report.

1. Probable asphyxia.
2. Vaginal sharp force injuries with interstitial hemorrhage.
3. Prolonged burial with postmortem changes.
4. Positive dental identification.
5. The manner of death is homicide.

By 2:30 PM, I was enroute to Warsaw. I needed to develop the photographs and write reports. More evidence came in. Undersheriff Ely handed over three shovels that Bruno had given him that morning. The grandfather had located three shovels around the trailer. Two had been in different locations outside the trailer, and one was in a toolshed near it. We needed to compare the soil still on the shovel blades with the burial area and the area around where the shovels were located. One or more of them could have been used to bury Samantha.

Sunday, May 25, 1997

I began my workday with another trip to Hermitage. Soil samples from the gravesite, the attempted hole in the woods, and one from soil in front of the tool shed were taken. I secured them in the evidence room along with the shovels, which would be taken to the crime lab after the Memorial Day holiday.

Rachel wanted to see her daughter. News reports had intimated that the body was in a well-preserved condition, and it was a natural request. She went to the medical examiner's office with her attorney, expecting that the staff would show her the body, so she could confirm it was her daughter. The ME's office called the coroner to let him know. There were a couple of problems. The ME had no viewing room, and although the body was preserved well enough for forensic findings, it was not for viewing. Mike met for some time with Rachel and her attorney to explain the situation, finally talking her out of the request.

Wednesday, May 28, 1997

The investigative team had had several conversations over the previous weeks about what Samantha might have eaten prior to the initial report of her disappearance. I had picked up a school menu in February from Karen Almeter, Letchworth's cafeteria manager. She'd stated then that we could take any food items we might need anytime down the road. We were going to need the school district's help now.

The stomach contents collected during the autopsy were dark brown and pasty with what looked like bean skins. I was aware of Dr. Michael Baden's work; he was a celebrated forensic expert in using stomach contents to help determine a time of death. We needed to know for certain what food remained in Samantha's stomach to learn more about her time of death, which was key in building the case against her murderer.

The superintendent, elementary principal, high school principal, business manager, and Mrs. Almeter met with me early Wednesday morning. I explained that we needed find out if any lunch items served on February 25 matched the stomach contents as reported in the preliminary autopsy findings. The menu for February was on the table, and we read off the different items. Breakfast for the day included choices of cornflakes, cowboy breakfast cake, chilled peaches, and milk. Lunch offered one choice between three entrées: macaroni and cheese with bread, bologna and cheese, or a peanut butter sandwich. Then children could select one or two choices from these foods: baked beans, chilled pineapple, turkey rice soup, or chocolate pudding, plus milk for a beverage.

Now that we had confirmed beans had been served on February 25, we needed to determine if the stomach contents were consistent with the school lunch. Grateful for the school's cooperation, which would speed up the process, I went with the cafeteria manager to collect samples of the beans. I secured an unopened #10 can of baked beans, along with a sample of uncooked beans in a container. All the beans were the exact brand served on February 25. Staff went ahead and prepared the beans as they normally did while I waited. They added brown sugar and molasses to a #10 can of beans and then baked it for ninety minutes at 350 degrees. Once all the samples were taken, I drove to the crime lab to drop off them with Dr. Jeanne Beno for testing. She was the Chief Toxicologist for the lab and a tireless advocate for victims of crime.

Thursday, May 29, 1997

We were anxious about the bean analysis and had numerous conversations and meetings throughout the day before reaching out to Dr. Baden. At the time, he was the Director of the Forensic Scientists for the NYS Police Crime Lab. He was certified as an anatomic pathologist, clinical pathologist, and forensic pathologist. We needed his expertise and wanted to lock him in as our expert witness before Colon's defense team did. Dr. Baden was in great demand, and we knew he might not be available. We were ecstatic when he agreed to meet with us on May 30 and fit us into his schedule. He had commitments in Albany in the morning and planned to fly out to Kansas City on another case later that day. If we could arrive first thing in the morning, he promised to give us a couple of hours of his time. DA Jerry Stout and I sat down to discuss what I would present to the pathologist the following day. Photographs needed to be organized, and I had a presentation to prepare.

While we were excited about Dr. Baden, the investigative team also had the sad duty to attend a memorial service at Letchworth Central School. Family members, school officials, and parents all joined the elementary students in remembering the smiling girl. Some read tributes to Samantha's short life, and the high school band played. A sundial was given in her memory and was to be placed in the school's courtyard. The solemn gathering once again brought home the searing reality of an innocent girl's life snuffed out way before her time.

Friday, May 30, 1997

FBI agents Runnels and Doktor joined me for the trip to Albany early in the morning. Shortly into the drive, we received a call from Dr. Baden. He was leaving Albany earlier than expected, and we needed to get there as soon as we could. I wasn't going to miss the opportunity to speak with him, so needless to say, it was a memorable trip for all of us—especially for Special Agent Doktor. He stated it was the quickest trip to Albany he'd ever experienced, and he looked relieved to get out of the car. I don't think he was willing to ride with me again after that day.

We arrived in time and were able to meet with Dr. Baden, Major Timothy McAuliffe, and a group of investigators of the New York State Police. My presentation to the group covered the investigation from the first day up to the present time. The FBI agents offered their accounts as well, along with their concerns. It was immediately apparent to me that Dr. Baden was genuinely interested in helping us and very approachable. He felt we were on the right track in using the stomach contents to help pinpoint the time of death. It was a real relief to know that he would help us. He would meet with Dr. Smith in Rochester and reexamine the body the following week.

Noel Zaldivar once again made an appearance in Wyoming County along with his mother and sister. Bruno took the lead in trying to arrange for local services, and Rachel was adamant that there would be no services until Samantha's body was released. The media reported that Noel's preference was to have his daughter buried in Wyoming County where she was known and people cared about her. But Rachel had other plans, which were to inter her in Georgia, near Angel's family. Although a memorial service at the funeral home in Warsaw was scheduled along with a mass at St. Michael's just down the street, both were postponed by the family. *The Daily News* reported that a memorial service would be held on Sunday, June 1 at the New Beginnings church in Hermitage.

The case against Colon was percolating furiously with the preliminary autopsy findings. Jerry Stout asked Colon— through his attorney Murray to submit samples of his pubic hair and blood. Murray told the DA that his client would cooperate if certain conditions were met. They wanted Bruno Stra to submit samples before Colon would agree to anything, and Wyoming County would have to provide transportation for Colon from Florida. Stout responded that others had already submitted blood and hair samples early in the case, as was quite routine. Colon hadn't provided the samples requested then, and it appeared he wasn't going to now. Colon also had plenty of legal problems in Florida, according to Monroe County authorities in south Florida. In addition to his arrest on several outstanding warrants, he had three probation violations and a rap sheet that included alleged felony auto theft.

Wednesday, June 4, 1997

Dr. Baden arrived at the medical examiner's office in Rochester for the second autopsy. DA Stout, Investigator Eck, Undersheriff Ely, and I traveled up to be present as well. Dr. Baden had reviewed all the materials we'd given him previously, and after meeting with Dr. Smith, another autopsy was performed that lasted four to five hours.

Dr. Baden's report would agree with Dr. Beno's findings that the bean casings were similar to the comparisons I had collected. He also confirmed the bean casings were similar to the small amount of remains found in the stomach and those served at the school.

When a person dies, all digestion ceases. Normally, the stomach empties out in three to four hours, depending on the type of food eaten. The stomach lining has ridges and grooves that retain some of the food even when the stomach empties. If there was another meal eaten, the remaining material more than likely would have been washed out. Dr. Baden believed the lunch meal had been Samantha's last meal since the vegetable material was still intact and had not been washed out by another meal. There was no evidence of additional food in her stomach after the school lunch. The time of death was consistent with the report of a scream at 8:30 PM the night of February 25 and not with Samantha being alive at 7:00 AM the next day. The bottom line—Samantha was murdered the evening of February 25 and never went out the door to the bus the morning of February 26.

Dr. Baden's findings revealed she'd died from traumatic asphyxia, which means some unnatural traumatic situation occurred where she couldn't breathe. He felt that some obstruction had been placed over her nose and mouth, such as a hand or pillow. This could not have been an accident as with an adult inadvertently rolling on top of a baby while sleeping. A seven-year-old would certainly wake up and move away in that situation. He also believed that it would take at least a minute or longer to keep pressure on the nose and mouth to asphyxiate her. The act had to be deliberate—intentional.

Dr. Baden's findings contradicted Dr. Smith's initial conclusion that he'd discussed in meetings that the asphyxiation could have been an unintentional outcome—accidental. This became a great concern for DA Stout. What could be proved beyond a reasonable doubt in court? Over the next few weeks, Dr. Smith reexamined all of the laboratory tests, and on July 29, made a correction on his preliminary report. He identified the immediate cause of death as probable asphyxia and not accidental.

Dr. Baden concurred with Dr. Smith's report that Samantha sustained severe injuries to the vaginal area. There were also small cuts or breaks in the vaginal lining. His opinion was that she had been sexually assaulted, and a finger or fingers could have caused the smaller breaks in the vaginal wall. However, the penis could not be excluded because of the type of injuries. It was sickening news.

Colon's Bronco. Used by permission of WCSO.

Stra Trailer: Rugs taken as evidence.
Used by permission of WCSO.

Stra Trailer. Used by permission of WCSO.

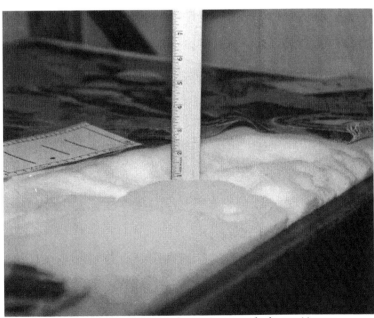

Missing piece of foam from Samantha's mattress.
Used by permission of WCSO.

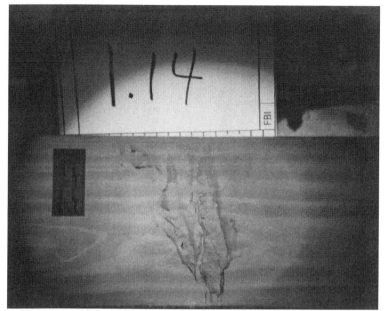

Alternate Light Source (ALS) shows bloodstain on bedrail.
Used by permission of WCSO.

Site of attempted grave. Used by permission of WCSO.

Aerial view of gravesite showing proximity to trailer park.
Used by permission of WCSO.

Aerial view of gravesite. Used by permission of the WCSO.

Conrad tractor and plow. Used by permission of WCSO.

L to R: Ron Ely, Paul Donnelly, Stephen Tarbell, David Davis, Gary
Eck. Florida Investigative Trip June 1997

Samantha Zaldivar, Christmas 1996.
Used by permission of Lisa Johnson.

Dennis Spink and Ron Ely lead Angel Colon out of the Wyoming
County Courthouse after Colon pleads guilty to second-degree murder.
Used by permission of *The Daily News*, Batavia, NY, August 14, 1998
Paul Mrozek photo.

CHAPTER 16

Thursday, June 5 – Tuesday, June 10, 1997

Days raced on as I reorganized evidence at the sheriff's office and transported several items to the crime lab for analysis. In 1997, I made forty-two trips to the crime lab. In all, more than one thousand pieces of evidence for this case would be logged in that were cataloged and organized so that they could be located at any time. Investigators were also talking about another trip, this time to Florida. We needed to locate Colon's family and friends and find out as much as we could about him. We had a lot of territory to cover, many individuals to interview, and we needed to use our time wisely; an effective plan was crucial. In a stroke of rare good luck, we put in a call to the Monroe County Sheriff's Department in Key West, Florida, where we knew one of the detectives. Mark Whitton, who was a former Warsaw Police officer, had also worked for the sheriff's department. He was now a detective in Key West. We all knew Mark well, and he was eager to assist in any way he could. He would make navigating the islands and locating individuals easier, and we could use his office when needed. Now that we had a trusted resource in Florida, the trip quickly came together.

Jerry Stout knew he had a possible death penalty case if he could get an indictment against Colon. New York State had reinstituted the death penalty for the most heinous crimes in 1995. The complexity of trying a capital murder case with the limited resources both monetarily and personnel-wise was staggering for the DA's office. Even though reimbursement of costs would come through the state, the county would foot the bill until the check came from Albany. A two-to three-million-dollar price tag was estimated. Jerry was the only full-time employee, and he had two part-time assistant DAs. He knew that his full attention had to be focused on the Zaldivar case, and adjustments in staffing had to happen. The board of supervisors agreed, and the part-timers were made full-time. Two more part-time assistant district attorneys were added as well. He also asked for assistance from NYS Attorney General, Dennis Vacco. The anticipated flurry of defense motions to answer and the demands of preparing evidence were beyond a solo prosecutor's capabilities. He would soon receive help from the Capital Assistance for Prosecutors team, headed by Diane LaVallee. LaVallee, who was the former head of the Sex Crimes Unit for the Erie County District Attorney's office in Buffalo, had taken a job with the AG's office earlier in the year. The AG sent the seasoned prosecutor back to Western New York along with her investigator, Harry Frank, to provide the support necessary to prosecute the case. Diane and Harry quickly proved themselves to be essential team members in preparing the case for trial.

The defense was ramping up their muscle as well. The NYS Capital Defenders Office sent a team to assist Norman Effman, Wyoming County Public Defender, and D. Michael Murray. Thomas Dunn and Patricia Warth would later take seats at the defense table.

One of the biggest concerns about building the case against Colon was the sentencing phase of the trial. Because it was a possible death penalty case, the defense had the right to bring out any mitigating factors. Mitigating factors encompassed the life of the defendant, especially his childhood. Any background information on him would help prepare the prosecution's case. We also needed to learn all we could about Samantha—where she was born, what statements from teachers, doctors, and school psychologists could tell us, and whether she'd participated in any church activities such as taking First Communion. We had a lot of ground to cover—both geographically and topically in Florida.

Wednesday, June 11 – Friday, June 13, 1997

Investigator Dave Davis and I headed for Florida by car on Wednesday afternoon. We arrived in the Ft. Lauderdale/Hollywood, Florida area on Thursday evening. Sore back muscles were stretched as we got out of the car. Thankfully, the marathon trip was at an end, and the two of us carried suitcases into the motel's office where we checked in. The 1,412-mile trip had taken us to only the first of several destinations we had to investigate.

Investigators Paul Donnelly and Gary Eck, who were with Undersheriff Ely, all traveled to the state of Georgia. They planned to attend the funeral services for Samantha at the Carson/Riverside Funeral Home in Valdosta. Some of Colon's family resided in the area, which seemed to be a peculiar place for the little girl's final resting place. However, word around Wyoming County was that Rachel intended to move back to Georgia to join Colon once again, which meant that Samantha's grave would be close by. The trio attended the service and went to the gravesite on Friday, taking a close look at who attended. Angel Colon was nowhere to be seen.

Dave Davis and I went to work on Friday, conducting interviews with people who knew Colon. Over the next eleven days, we scoured neighborhoods, tracking down individuals with a connection to him. We had no evidence that linked anyone else to the crime other than Angel Colon, but we needed sufficient evidence to charge him with Samantha's murder. We were still awaiting final autopsy and lab results on the evidence. It was imperative that we begin the task of gathering information to help us sort through the mitigating factors the defense was sure to use if we did indeed charge him. He had relatives and friends throughout Florida. Prior to moving to New York, he'd resided in Miami and Key West. His whereabouts were unknown since he had fled New York, but the latest information indicated that Colon was living in Marathon, Florida.

Our interviews over the next few days gave us the framework of what Samantha's life in Florida had been like. Routine doctor visits were in the records of a pediatric clinic, and we found the school she had attended. It took a few tries before we were able to talk with the principal and her teacher since the schools were on summer break. But once we connected, we found that Samantha had been a happy and energetic student—cooperative and helpful in class. She had been bilingual and helped Spanish-speaking students who didn't know English.

We attended Mass at Our Lady Queen of Heaven Catholic Church in North Lauderdale so we could talk with the priest after the service. He didn't remember the family and directed us to the parish office for information. The office staff didn't have any information on them either. Samantha, her mother, and sisters hadn't been all that visible in the community, although an apartment complex manager talked about Rachel being in an abusive relationship with a husband or boyfriend. Rachel's mother Ruth Velarde had offered the information to the manager at the time the family had lived there. Ruth had also put down the deposit for an apartment to help Rachel find a safer environment. All of this had happened in 1995. The manager also remembered missing posters being distributed in the area when Samantha first disappeared. The manager assumed that the Zaldivar family probably dropped them off. The tenants' high turnover rate meant that there were no occupants at the complex who'd lived there when Rachel and her daughters had. We moved on.

We began going door-to-door at another apartment complex, trying to gain any new information about Angel, Rachel, or Samantha. As expected, some were cooperative, and others were blatantly anti-police. Word traveled quickly around the complex that the police were asking about Colon. After deciding that we'd exhausted any leads there, we climbed back into our unmarked vehicle to leave. As I put the car in reverse and started backing out of the driveway, we were startled by a loud noise, which made me immediately jam it into park. We all got out and examined underneath the car and the area around it. The source of the clanking was easily found. A small metal pipe with a pointed end had been wedged underneath one of the rear tires in an attempt to cause damage. Lucky for us when we backed up, the pipe dropped harmlessly onto the concrete and didn't puncture the tire.

Over the next several days, we parked in different areas as we continued to canvass neighborhoods where Colon had lived. After discussing the situation with the Miami police, they recommended a heightened police presence and began guarding our vehicles in their marked cars as we attempted more interviews.

Tuesday, June 17, 1997

A call came in the evening of June 17, informing us that the Town of Wethersfield Justice Court had issued a warrant for the arrest of Angel Colon on the charges stemming from the March incident when Angela and Cassandra had been removed from the trailer by social services. He hadn't appeared in town court to answer the charges of resisting arrest and obstructing governmental administration. As soon as we received the news, we immediately conducted surveillance on a residence where he'd been seen along with some other promising areas. He wasn't sighted. He was keeping a low profile, and we assumed he knew we were asking about his whereabouts.

The next day, we learned that Angel was on probation with the state of Florida and attempted to contact his probation officer. We had no luck getting a response from the probation department and continued to track down relatives who might know where he was. Some stated that even if they knew where he was, they wouldn't tell us. There were plenty of opinions about whether Angel was guilty of the murder or if Bruno Stra was involved. Some were reluctant to cooperate with us out of fear of retaliation from Angel. The apprehension on their faces told us plenty.

Thursday, June 19, 1997

I accompanied Undersheriff Ely to re-interview the Zaldivar family, specifically Noel, Samantha's father, and Lucely, Noel's sister. Lucely and Rachel had known each other since 1988, and the ex-sister-in-law had seen the lifestyle that Samantha had experienced of moving around between family members. She believed Rachel had had an affair with an employer and caused fighting between Noel and his brother Eloy. Samantha, who was born in 1990, seemed to be caught in a volatile family situation and was often left to fend for herself. It only worsened when Angel entered the picture after Rachel had divorced Noel. Lucely remembered talking with Noel about a call he'd received from a panicked Rachel. She and Angel had been kicked out of their apartment, and she needed a place to stay since Angel was beating her up. Noel, who was living with Lucely at the time, had asked his sister to allow Rachel and Samantha to stay with them. After agreeing to help out, Lucely found herself caring for Samantha when Rachel disappeared for two weeks.

In a big scene, Rachel returned with her mother to pick up Samantha. Noel refused to let his daughter go at first, but finally acquiesced when Velarde threatened to have him arrested.

Later on, Rachel showed up at Lucely's workplace to let her know that she'd left Angel because of his drug use and abuse. He'd stolen from her and the girls to buy more drugs. Her mother had helped with an apartment and car for her. A job waiting tables at a Denny's had helped stabilize the home life, and Lucely thought Rachel was finally doing better. Lucely didn't see Rachel again until after Angela and Cassandra were born. The last time she'd seen her former sister-in-law was in March 1997 when she and Noel traveled to Wyoming County.

Noel's account of his relationship and marriage with Rachel was similar to his sister's statement. Her continuing affair with his brother Eloy had angered him, and when the divorce was finalized, he'd been depressed over the breakup. However, he'd taken Rachel's roommate to Mexico for about a month. When they returned to the United States, he was told that Rachel was living with Colon at Colon's mother's place in North Miami. It was at this point he realized that reconciliation with her was impossible. This was in July 1992, according to his recollection. He had intermittent contact with Rachel after that, usually because of problems with Angel. Then he received the phone call from Samantha in December 1996, prompted by Samantha's maternal grandmother. It was last time he'd talked with his daughter. He'd learned of her disappearance in February 1997 and had come to New York with his sister.

Friday, June 20 – Saturday, June 21, 1997

Rachel's mother Ruth was re-interviewed, and she shared her dislike of Colon with us. She felt he had led her daughter into a life of poverty and drugs, and she'd done her best to help Rachel get away from him, but to no avail. She'd feared for Samantha's safety with Angel in the house. When she'd received the call from her other daughter Alexandria, who told her Samantha was missing, she'd immediately made plans to fly to Buffalo. Angel had called her around midnight of March 1, just a few hours before their flight. He told Ruth not to come because it would make things look bad for him.

Ruth had informed him that she was coming to Hermitage to see Rachel and her granddaughters, not him. She'd also asked him if he knew what had happened to Samantha, much to his irritation. He responded that he'd last seen her going out the door to the bus, which angered Velarde because he hadn't walked her to the bus.

Her interaction with Angel and Rachel didn't seem to go much better once she arrived at the trailer in Hermitage. Angel was defensive and angry, telling her not to ask Rachel questions about Samantha. Her last comment in the interview was, "I got the chills from him looking at me."

Investigator Paul Donnelly and I left the apartment in Pembroke Pines more determined than ever to find Angel Colon.

On Saturday, Detective Mark Whitton joined Investigator Dave Davis and me for a visit to a trailer park in Marathon. We planned to go door-to-door in an attempt to ascertain Colon's whereabouts. There were several people who didn't know him at all, but others were familiar with him. A couple of residents said they remembered seeing Angel around the trailer park about a month earlier. Then we talked with a woman who said she'd seen him ten days prior and that he'd been with a woman who lived in the mobile home park.

Once we located this woman, she admitted that Angel had lived at her home for a time since leaving New York State. She appeared to be very nervous and reluctant to speak with us. She did mention that Angel had attended the funeral in Georgia on June 13, which we knew wasn't true, and had called her the next day to let her know he was in the Miami area.

After a couple of additional interviews with people who'd seen Colon a month ago, we knocked on the door of an elderly woman named Bertha. As soon as Angel Colon was mentioned, she became agitated and nervous. She took a step backward and started to slap her cheek with her left hand.

"No, no, no," she said, shaking her head.

We learned that she had more than eighteen great-grandchildren and six grandchildren. She stated emphatically that she didn't want any trouble and directed us back to the woman Colon had been staying with. Our impression was that Bertha was fearful of Angel, but for what reason—she wouldn't elaborate. She kept repeating, "I have to worry about my own grandchildren."

After leaving the trailer court, we drove to Keys Fisheries in Marathon. We were hoping to find Colon working on the fishing boats as he'd previously told his attorney. We spoke with the foreman in charge that day, who immediately said that he'd never heard of him. He suggested that we check with other fisheries in the area, which we did.

We searched the waterway in the hot, afternoon Florida sun until we located a captain of a fishing boat who said he'd almost hired Angel. The seawater lapped against the docks, and the strong odor of fish and saltwater stung my nose. I wiped the sweat from my forehead, wishing for a cold drink.

The captain readily shared that he'd given him a job in April, but Colon hadn't shown up because of a motorcycle accident. At least that's what Colon said when he called the captain. When he received some type of official paperwork asking how much money Angel would have made if he was fishing, the captain tore it up and threw it away. He hadn't seen or heard from Colon since. It seemed that he'd vanished.

CHAPTER 17

July 1997

After we returned home, the legal side of the case began to heat up. We still needed Colon's blood and hair samples. With a warrant for his arrest from the Wethersfield Justice Court, there was a way to get him back to New York, but he'd dropped out of sight. I attended several meetings with the District Attorney's office, the medical examiner's office, and the other law enforcement agencies to solidify the case so it could go forward against Angel.

The District Attorney's office had contacted the U.S. Marshals in Florida to talk about the possibility of gaining their assistance in tracking him down. Much time was spent in meetings, reviewing reports of evidence analysis by the Monroe County Crime Lab with the multi-agency taskforce, and discussing the strength of the case against Colon. Jerry Stout was moving ahead with the case to present it to the grand jury. It was crucial to get the charges right, which would increase the chances of an indictment being handed down by the grand jury.

Other cases continued to pile up that month, including a burglary and an attempted rape. I was at each scene, collecting evidence and taking photos. I also served subpoenas to witnesses being called to testify at the grand jury scheduled at the end of the month.

Friday, July 18, 1997

The U.S. Marshal's Office, along with Miami and Metro Dade County police, had found Angel Colon. The other piece of good news was they hadn't charged the county for their services, which helped our budget. He was arrested and taken into custody without any trouble around 6:30 PM. The unanswered misdemeanor charges in Justice Court had been his snare. They'd located him at a friend's residence in Homestead, Florida, and the 23-year-old was now sitting in a Miami jail. We finally had him within reach, and extradition to New York was the next step.

Colon was arraigned before a federal magistrate where he decided to fight extradition to New York. The charges were misdemeanors and not worthy of coming back to New York, D. Michael Murray told the press. He went on to say that he'd never seen it happen in his career as a defense attorney. Now DA Stout would have to obtain a letter from New York State Governor George Pataki, stating that Colon was a wanted individual in New York and then a Florida judge would determine if Colon would be sent back to us. It wasn't a speedy process and could take a month or more.

The DA wasn't backing down and planned to go ahead to haul Colon back to Wyoming County to face the charges. The analysis of the forensic evidence was almost complete in the case, and Jerry told the media he was about ready to name a suspect. Murray was determined to keep Colon in Florida for as long as legally possible. Other rumors were flying that Rachel had been granted immunity in the case, which the DA quickly quashed; however, he said it had been discussed with her attorney.

The very real possibility that Rachel could be charged in connection with Samantha's murder prompted her public defender attorney, Anthony Irrera, to request help from the state's Capital Defenders Office in Rochester. The press had interviewed him, and his fear was that the evidence we had was enough to support an indictment against his client as an accomplice to the murder or at the very least a charge of assisting in the removal of her daughter's body. Rachel hadn't been available to us for any further interviews for weeks by her attorney's orders, and we knew the pressure was on her. Jerry Stout and Diane LaVallee felt strongly that she was the key to the case, and this move was an indication her attorney felt the same way.

The complexity of Rachel's defense was growing with further charges in Family Court against her and Colon for sexual abuse of Samantha, Angela, and Cassandra. Irrera's request was granted, and Paul J. Cambria, Jr., a top defense attorney from Buffalo, NY, was appointed to assist him.

Thursday, July 31, 1997

The grand jury met at the Wyoming County Courthouse, and a line of witnesses took their turn inside with Jerry Stout asking the questions before the jurors. A list of nineteen counts was presented to them, all against Angel Colon. There were four counts of first-degree murder, eight counts of second-degree murder, six counts of sexual abuse, and one count of endangering the welfare of a child. I was one of the witnesses that day presenting evidence, as were Dr. Baden, Bruno Stra, FBI agents, and Wyoming County Sheriff Investigators. In grand jury proceedings, the district attorney presents his case without the defense being present. After I left the room, I had a sense of relief. I believed the case was solid. Our evidence was good, and we had top-notch experts to support the forensic findings. I was confident Angel Colon would be indicted on all counts.

Thursday, August 7, 1997

The grand jury handed down its nineteen-count indictment against Angel Colon. The jurors had agreed with the District Attorney on every count. There was some celebration when we heard the news. The long hours and painstaking effort in collecting evidence and countless interviews with family, neighbors, and so many others had paid off. The extradition holdup would most certainly evaporate with these charges.

Colon's public defender, Norm Effman, began talking to the DA about the defendant's inevitable return to Wyoming County. Effman was extremely concerned that Colon might make a casual confession to Wyoming County officers if they transported him back from the South. If that occurred, it could absolutely be used at trial. Now that there was a murder indictment, he had all the more reasons to protect his client's rights, which was why he insisted that one member of the defense team accompany Colon during the transport if the U.S. Marshals couldn't bring him to New York. Jerry Stout had no objection to the defense's request, which was reasonable and not out of the ordinary.

Norman Effman has been the Wyoming County Public Defender since 1990. Well-respected in the legal and law-enforcement communities, we knew he would present a vigorous defense for his client. I personally knew that he would go by the book, and I had and have a great deal of respect for him. His curriculum vitae is impressive. Not only was he the public defender, but he was the executive director of the Wyoming County-Attica Legal Aid Bureau, which conducted litigation for prisoners' rights, most of whom were incarcerated in New York's notorious Attica prison facility. He was a grad of the University of Buffalo Law School and had received prestigious awards for his outstanding service as a criminal defense attorney. He served on the Attorney Grievance Committee of the Appellate Division and other committees. Two other attorneys from the Capital Defenders Office were now part of the team too. Patricia Warth and Thomas Dunn would lend their expertise.

The prosecution team of Stout and LaVallee were not out of their league going toe-to-toe with the defense. Jerry was a Syracuse University School of Law grad, and Diane had earned her Juris Doctor from the University of Buffalo. Stout had been in private practice for twenty-two years with well-known Charlotte Smallwood-Cook. Their offices had been in the elegant converted Victorian home with a signature fountain across the street from the Wyoming County Courthouse. He had begun his tenure as Wyoming County District Attorney in a part-time position that had grown into a full-time responsibility. His skill in the courtroom and integrity had earned him the respect of law enforcement and defense counsel alike. The people of Wyoming County placed their confidence in him and elected him to the position multiple times until his retirement in 2011. He served twenty years as district attorney with an additional eight years as a part-time DA and now enjoys a well-deserved retirement.

Diane was a formidable prosecutor, and earlier in 1997, had earned the position of Chief on the Attorney General's Capital Assistance to Prosecutors Unit. Her credentials were impeccable, and she often taught at NYS Bar seminars and at her alma mater, the University of Buffalo. She was also a founding member of Erie County's Child Advocacy Center and Child Fatality Review Team. Today, she continues to work in the NYS Attorney General's Office as Deputy Bureau Chief in the Special Investigations Unit and as an Assistant Attorney General in Criminal Enforcement and Financial Crimes Bureau.

The possibility that Jerry would seek the death penalty in the case had all of us on edge. Everything must be done perfectly and according to the rules. Every motion and every piece of evidence would scrutinized by the defense for an appeal if he was convicted. There was no room for error.

Jerry hoped that the U.S. Marshal's Service would be able to transport Colon to Warsaw. We had our fingers crossed that it would facilitate the extradition. There was also a cost consideration. If federal authorities delivered him, it would save Wyoming County taxpayers some money. Logistical issues were still a problem though; Angel's court date of August 20 in Florida was a Wednesday, and the marshals transported prisoners on Tuesday. The paperwork would probably not be completed by the following week. Negotiations continued between the lawyers.

Friday, August 8 – Tuesday, August 19, 1997

Ultimately, the defense team and Colon decided not to fight extradition. The prosecution and defense had come to terms on his transportation. Although Wyoming County Sheriff's personnel would transport him, a defense attorney would accompany them. Arrangements would take time, and it looked like early September was the soonest he would return. I was anxious that he be arraigned, as was everyone else. Justice needed to happen for Samantha. The final pieces of the puzzle—at least most of them—were finally falling into place.

Although Diane LaVallee had been assisting the DA's office, Stout officially requested to have her appointed as an assistant district attorney. He made his request to Judge Mark H. Dadd, and it was granted. She was then sworn in as a Wyoming County Special Assistant District Attorney.

The prosecution team went forward, and Jerry filed a notice with the Capital Defender's Office that he might seek the death penalty against Colon.

Friday, September 5, 1997

I had a shopping trip to make while Gary Eck and Ron Ely were preparing to fly to Florida. Samantha's stomach contents were crucial to the case, pinpointing her time of death. I visited a grocery store in Warsaw to pick up two cans each of several different kinds of beans to be compared with those that had been found in the stomach contents. With ten cans of beans on the front seat, I headed back to the Monroe County Crime Lab to turn them over to Dr. Beno. She would do the testing and also had a toxicology report ready for me to pick up. We needed to know for certain that no other canned beans could have been in her stomach. If they didn't match the school's bean recipe, then the time of death could have been completely different. The lab also returned twenty-one pieces of evidence to me to be secured in our evidence room. These were from Samantha's bedroom and from the Bronco.

Saturday, September 6, 1997 - Monday, September 8, 1997

Sergeant Investigator Gary Eck and Undersheriff Ron Ely left the Buffalo airport for Miami. Their responsibility was to escort Colon back to Warsaw. Gary's memories of that trip are still vivid. Their flight was at 10:20 AM and took them through Detroit before landing in Miami around 3:06 PM. Patricia Warth, a member of the defense team, accompanied them. She would ensure that Colon kept his mouth shut on the way back. On Monday, September 8, the undersheriff and investigator met with Miami-Dade officers, who handed Colon over to them. He was dressed in a typical orange jumpsuit, which raised Warth's ire. He would certainly be conspicuous, and that was something she wanted to avoid. She had expected him to be dressed in a suit. Because of flight times and the unavailability of a change of street clothes, the entourage headed for the airport.

The trip back was much more dramatic and disconcerting. Word had leaked out Colon was being extradited that day, and when they arrived at the Miami airport, a contingent of angry protesters met the group inside. They were carrying placards with "Child Killer" handwritten on them, shouting their condemnation of Colon as the group hustled him toward the gate. Airport personnel jumped in to help get them aboard the aircraft ahead of everyone else. Gary remembers that they'd sat ten or fifteen minutes on the plane before a few other passengers straggled on. The pilot and a couple of other officials walked to the back of the plane where they were seated and told them there was a problem. Passengers had witnessed the demonstration and were worried about their safety. The officials asked if Colon could be taken on a later flight, which was about three hours later.

Eck and Ely had no desire to stay an additional three hours in the airport with a prisoner and angry demonstrators. They intended to remain on the plane—they had their tickets and couldn't be removed. Airport officials had to agree, and a few minutes later, a handful of passengers nervously walked on board, but the flight wasn't by any means a full one. The route back went through Detroit again, where they boarded a smaller prop aircraft and arrived back in Buffalo a little after 6:00 PM. Warth had made arrangements with her team for a set of clothes to be brought to the airport, and Colon was able to change on the aircraft before they deplaned.

The media flocked around them with reporters trying to get a comment from anyone, but the group ignored their pleas and hurried to the parking lot. Warth clutched her client's right arm, with Ely on his left, and Gary followed directly behind Colon. A jacket was draped over Colon's hands to hide the handcuffs. Bruno Stra was in the crowd, watching with tear-filled eyes as his granddaughter's killer was put in the back of a patrol car.

CHAPTER 18

Tuesday, September 9, 1997

Angel Colon stood before the Hon. Mark H. Dadd to hear the charges against him—first-degree murder, second-degree murder, sexual abuse, and endangering the welfare of a child. The defense table was crowded with Colon and his four attorneys. He pled not guilty to the nineteen counts, which surprised no one. No bail was set, and he was remanded to the county jail as anticipated. The DA would have fifteen days to file any additional paperwork with the court, and then the defense would examine it and respond. Jerry was ready to go to trial, having already filed a statement of readiness for trial and a demand for Colon's alibi—if he had one. These were all routine filings, and we knew a trial date was far off in the future.

The courtroom was packed, full of the press and onlookers. Maria Padilla, Samantha's paternal grandmother, was crying as she held photos of Samantha. Bruno was also present, as was his girlfriend Lisa Johnson, to hear the charges read. Emotions were high for everyone, seeing Colon having to face the music. We had a great deal of concern over Colon's safety as he did the "perp walk" from the jail to the courthouse and up the stairs to the courtroom. Cameras were everywhere. Ely and those accompanying him were extra vigilant that day. A small group of protesters called Movement Opposing Molesters demonstrated on the sidewalk outside the courthouse, yelling out to motorists to honk their horns to support Samantha. They shouted out, "child killer" for all to hear as they raised their signs in the air.

Colon appeared emotionless during the brief proceedings, and his defense team had already filed an order to show cause with the Appellate Division over Judge Dadd's appointment of Diane LaVallee. The defense contended in its civil action that the governor should have been the one to appoint her. It was a procedural matter and was expected by the prosecution. Jerry was unconcerned and told reporters there was no merit to the action, but it would have to play out in the system. Although the litigation was customary, Norm Effman reflected on the case that it was one that required "the most expert people involved on both ends for any semblance of justice to occur." He had a great deal of respect for Jerry and Diane, but he had a vigorous defense to present for his client. He was also walking a procedural tightrope and didn't want to make any missteps in his defense of Colon.

Big decisions were ahead, and if Jerry was going to seek the death penalty, he had 120 days to come to a determination. He was in no hurry and wanted the time to consider the evidence we had and every facet of the case before pursuing it.

Samantha's murder was categorized as felony murder, which meant another crime was committed during the murder. He would have to prove beyond a reasonable doubt that Angel had intended to murder Samantha. There was some easing of the workload for the sheriff's department now that the case was firmly in the hands of the lawyers. But there was more evidence that required analysis, plus we still needed the blood and hair samples from Colon himself. Plenty of other cases would keep me on the run in October and November.

Thursday, September 11 – Sunday, September 21, 1997

A serious motor vehicle accident (MVA) drew my attention on September 11. There were injuries, and I was there to photograph and process the scene. Then on September 19, a fatal MVA claimed the life of a Monroe County Assistant DA's mother. The accident occurred in the Town of Pike, and I handled processing the scene there as well. The next day, I spent my birthday at the Monroe County Medical Examiner's office and cancelled the plans I had to celebrate. On Sunday, we had a report of a barn fire in the Town of Arcade, which we suspected was arson.

October 1997

When Samantha's body had been discovered in May, the FBI assistance evaporated. Because the case was a possible kidnapping, which was a federal crime, they had been able to help us. Now that it was a murder, they didn't have jurisdiction. It wasn't until Diane LaVallee brought in her investigator, Harold "Harry" Frank, that we had additional manpower for the continuing investigation. Harry, a Special Investigator for the New York Attorney General's Office, had begun his work by helping us prepare the evidence, photos, and statements for trial. He was impressed with the sheer amount of evidence that we had obtained and the mountain of statements. He plunged into the work and wanted to familiarize himself with the area, especially the trailer park, burial site, and woods. We spent a lot of time going over the now very familiar ground of Samantha's home and gravesite. He reviewed the reports on the autopsy and the stomach contents.

Harry had been with the City of Buffalo Police Department for twenty-seven years before joining the AG's team in Albany. Fifteen of those years he'd spent as a homicide detective, and he'd investigated many high-profile cases. When the death penalty was restored to the state, he was asked by the AG's office to come on board to assist with death penalty cases. He agreed, retiring from the Buffalo City Police Department. He now worked from the AG's office, headquartered in Albany. He'd previously teamed up with Diane LaVallee when she was the Assistant District Attorney in Erie County, and she had asked him to help us. He was familiar with Diane's prosecutorial style and method of working a case, as she was with his. It was an excellent team that was ready to give us a hand. He brought a fresh perspective to our work, and I was eager to have him assess our progress.

He dug into the statements that the Wyoming County investigators and the FBI had taken and told us we needed more than narrative statements from individuals. He recommended preparing direct questions, which would elicit direct answers, much like the attorneys would use in court. He evaluated our investigative plan and helped us prepare the questions for those we needed to re-interview. Item by item, he went through the evidence, determining what analysis was needed on which piece. Harry compiled information on what had already been done with evidence, what hadn't been tested, and if there were additional analysis needed on already analyzed items. He never took a negative approach to anything that had been done, but only a positive one. His easygoing personality and street smarts proved to be beneficial to us, and we were able to accomplish much more with his assistance. Many times Harry was riding with me while working on the Zaldivar case, and I would be dispatched to a burglary investigation, fire investigation, or occasionally the closest car was needed to help retrieve keys for a motorist from a locked vehicle. He never complained and pitched in to help. I believe the other investigators felt the same way about Investigator Frank, as he was a great guy and a pleasure to work with. He had one goal in mind as we did, and that was to bring justice to Samantha.

Friday, October 3, 1997

A call came from Director Rodwell at the crime lab that he wanted a couple of pieces of evidence returned for further analysis. They were Samantha's pink blanket and her pillow. Putting that delivery on my schedule for the following day, I went to meet with the MVA victim's family to explain the circumstances of the deadly crash.

Monday, October 6 – Tuesday, October 7, 1997

I returned the blanket and pillow to the lab on Monday, and then Undersheriff Ely asked Harry and me to see Lyle Drake and his daughter, Lisa Johnson at the trailer park in Hermitage.

The fall colors were almost at peak as Harry and I drove the quiet roads to Hermitage on Tuesday. The weather was pleasant, and it seemed hard to believe we'd been searching the fields and woods in frigid temperatures for Samantha just months before. So much had happened in the eight-month investigation, but there was a pile of work still to do to ensure that Samantha received a measure of justice.

Yellow-and-red leaves were scattered across yards in the trailer park when we drove in to meet Lyle. He was at a shed on the southwest end of the property. We continued to check out Colon's account of his movements over the days immediately preceding Samantha's disappearance as well as those days after, especially February 26 and 27. In question was the whereabouts of a battery Colon stated he'd taken from a shed in order to start the Bronco on February 26. After starting the Bronco he said he'd returned the battery to a BMW, but the battery was nowhere to be found in our earlier attempts to locate it. We needed to know if the battery actually existed or if the story was a fabrication in Colon's statement.

We began searching around the perimeter of the shed and then entered the building. Our eyes adjusted to the gloomy interior as we scanned the contents, and then began to comb through the tools and equipment. Harry and I poked around looking for the battery, unexpectedly spotting a shovel and ice chopper in a jumbled dark section of the building. When Harry lifted up the shovel, we immediately saw that there was soil adhered to the blade. A long-handled ice chopper sat next to it. Lyle was surprised to see the two implements. When asked previously if there were any other shovels around, he'd stated that there weren't. But these had been placed out of the way in the back of the shed behind a lawn tractor and were difficult to see. We decided to bag the items and take soil samples from the square-bladed shovel and ice chopper. They would be taken to the crime lab for comparison against the soil samples we'd collected from the gravesite and near the trailer. When you're looking for evidence, I learned early on it usually wasn't where you thought it would be, and you had to be slow, methodical, and persistent in searching.

I had previously collected three shovels near the trailer, and two had soil stuck to the blades. However, none matched the gravesite soil composition, but the samples had been similar to the soil around the shed and the trailer. I was hoping for different results in testing this newly discovered shovel.

Lisa arrived as we were bagging up the shovel to let us know she'd found the battery in the BMW that was parked alongside the shop. We learned that another individual had picked up the battery lying in the grass and put it back in the BMW. She noticed that there was some dark-colored substance on one of the battery posts. Lisa also told us that

Angel had returned a pair of work boots borrowed from Bruno during the early days of the search. When Bruno had picked up the boots, he'd found them wet from cleaning—even the grooves in the treads were immaculate.

She also told us about Angel's jackets—one was a Buffalo Bills jacket that Lisa's father Lyle had given him. He wore it only for work or when he was working outside and might get dirty. Angel also had a Miami Dolphins jacket that he wore socially. The Dolphins jacket had been a Christmas gift in 1996. We'd talked with the owner of the Hermitage General Store, who told us Angel had stopped in on February 25 to buy some gas and was wearing the Bills jacket. The Bills jacket was examined during the course of the investigation at the crime lab and no blood or soil connected to the gravesite was found. The jackets didn't yield any useful information about the case.

We took our lucky find of the shovel and ice chopper, along with the battery which we originally had gone out to locate that day. I delivered the items to the crime lab for a comparison analysis. I also resubmitted the soil samples from the gravesite, woods, and trailer area. Analysis would reveal that the soil on the square-bladed shovel was similar to the gravesite. If there were any other bits of evidence that would convict Samantha's killer, I wanted to find them.

The rest of the month of October was mainly focused on another high-profile case that was going to trial at the end of the month. We'd arrested the perpetrator in the home invasion case in the Town of Eagle, and there was extensive preparation to complete before the trial date. My Saturdays in October were spent with Investigator Dennis Spink and Assistant DA David DiMatteo, who was prosecuting the case. Subpoenas had to be served and evidence reviewed to make sure DiMatteo was ready. I testified twice at the home invasion trial, the last time on November 3. Then a house fire in Bennington followed by a church burglary investigation in the same township kept me buried in processing scenes in early November.

Friday, November 14, 1997

The prosecution had applied to the judge to obtain a court order to collect the blood and hair samples needed from Colon. I was happy to hear it had been granted. I arrived at the Wyoming County Jail that morning in snowy weather, which slowed travel for everyone. Jail personnel told me first thing that the defense attorney was running late because of road conditions. I met first with a registered nurse, who had two sexual assault kits for me to examine and two purple-topped tubes for blood sample collection. A few minutes later, defense counsel Thomas Dunn arrived. We talked briefly about the collection of the samples. He reminded me that no head hair samples were mentioned in the court order. Only pubic hairs and blood were specifically listed.

I asked him if the defense wanted its own samples of hair and blood, to which Dunn replied "no," while shaking his head. The jail's RN was standing next to Dunn, and I told her we would need a minimum of twenty-five pubic hairs and just two tubes of blood since the defense didn't require samples as well. Angel sat at the table while the nurse prepared his left arm, wiping the area with alcohol and then drawing the blood needed.

A doctor from the Wyoming County Community Hospital entered the room. He would be responsible for collecting the pubic hairs from six different sites, taking care that we had at least twenty-five to use at the lab. He was efficient in his work, and in a few minutes, the hair samples and tubes of blood were secured in the sexual assault kits. I placed the kits in a paper bag and taped them up with evidence tape and labeled the bag. Soon I was on my way back to the crime lab in Rochester with these long-sought samples. I believed they could be the final bit of evidence needed to convict Colon. The samples would be sent to NY State Police Lab for DNA testing. Pubic hairs had been discovered in Samantha's room—some from her pink blanket. They were not hers, nor were they from anyone else who had submitted blood and hair samples. We were looking for a match to the person who had committed her murder.

Three days later, I delivered the bucket seat from the Bronco back to the lab as requested. The lab director cut a control sample from the seat, which would also be sent to the NY State Police lab in Albany. I hoisted the bucket seat from the table and placed it in my vehicle for the return trip to the evidence room. It would be four to six weeks before DNA testing would be completed. Then it would have to be compared to the other samples we had. Inch by inch, we made progress.

December 1997

While the prosecution awaited the decision from the Appellate Court as to the validity of Diane LaVallee's appointment, the prosecution had filed its own objection with Judge Dadd about the size of the defense team. Four against two seemed unbalanced, and the motions between the lawyers continued to mount. The case was still in the discovery phase, each side requesting information from the other.

I was called to an arson fire at a commercial building in the Village of Perry and delved into that investigation, which would take several days. The Perry Police Department needed my help to determine if their suspicions about the fire were correct.

Late in the month, the Appellate Court ruled that LaVallee's appointment was okay although Judge Dadd had not issued a ruling on the size of the defense team.

Meetings were ongoing with the crime lab, which included the forensic chemists, the director, the medical examiner, Dr. Smith, and Dr. Beno. They continued the exacting task of going through all of the submitted samples, evaluating the results, determining what further testing would be needed, and requesting any additional items for testing.

While motions were flying back and forth between attorneys, I continued to work on a master catalog of the evidence for the case. The task of collecting evidence and keeping it organized was overwhelming to say the least. These were the days before we had database software to manage evidence. The Monroe County Crime Laboratory, which contracted with Wyoming County, also served all of Monroe County and at least sixty-six law enforcement agencies surrounding Monroe County at that time. We always prioritized what we needed to be processed at the crime lab because of the backlog. Cases that needed to be processed for court received precedence. In the first three months of this investigation, the FBI and our department collected hundreds of pieces of evidence. Every item had to be marked and tagged properly, then photographed and secured in an appropriate manner. At least 150 pieces of evidence had been taken to the crime lab for analysis, and hundreds had not. By the end of the first year of this investigation, we had close to a thousand pieces of evidence. Some departments might say that is no big deal, but our crime scene investigation unit was only one person.

After the recovery of Samantha's body, the investigative team started to prepare for a trial by organizing all of our evidence so that the prosecutors' job would be easier when the time came. When not occupied with any new or pending cases, we diligently worked on this process.

I was cataloging and cross-referencing each item that would be used at trial, according to Jerry's detailed instructions. I still remember it like it was yesterday. The job was so overwhelming that I wondered how in the hell I'd ever get it done.

He told me after meeting with Diane one day: "Say we've got the piece of foam with blood on it. That's evidence number one. I want a folder made up with how it was collected, the lab report for that, and any other pieces of evidence pertaining to the foam that we can relate it to ... I want those listed on the outside of the manila folder in numerical order and all the lab reports that go with those in that folder too." My eyes widened, and I took deep breath. Nodding, I rose from the chair in front of Jerry's desk and put on my game face. The work would get done.

After that meeting, the process went forward. Starting with evidence #1, I enclosed the reports on location of recovery, date, time, and lab report. Then I had to check evidence #1 to ascertain how that item compared to any other piece of evidence, e.g., evidence #29, #138, and #378. Finally those reports were attached to the file for evidence #1. Thus, we created a file for evidence #1 then went on to evidence #2. This was very time-consuming, but if we were going to end up in a trial, it would make life easier for everyone, including the defense team, with everything cross-referenced.

CHAPTER 19

January – April 1998

On January 2, Investigator Dennis Spink and Special Investigator Harry Frank went to re-interview Ada Fuller at the trailer park. She had more to say to investigators, but had been afraid of Angel Colon when she'd initially been interviewed the previous February. Now she wanted to fully recount all she'd heard the evening of February 25, 1997. Mrs. Fuller thought she'd heard Samantha shriek in pain between 8:30 and 9:00 PM and expected another scream after hearing it over the sound of her television. It sounded like it had come from the bathroom area of the trailer. She even poked her head out the front door of her own trailer, but nothing looked amiss next door. When she didn't hear another sound, the elderly woman resumed watching her usual TV programs. She was bothered about the type of scream she'd heard—it was different and troubling. Before she went to bed around 1:15 AM, she took another look at the Stra/Colon trailer. The lights were still on. Then when she was in bed, a few minutes later, she heard the sound of a vehicle starting up from the residence. The older woman didn't know that Rachel was away from home that evening. She told investigators that if she had been aware of Rachel's absence, she would have contacted Lisa Johnson to check on things.

The deadline for the DA came and went on the death penalty decision in January. Judge Dadd granted an extension and would grant another one. Deciding to pursue putting someone to death is not an easy decision. It was one that Jerry grappled with for many months and did not take lightly. Personally, he was not a proponent of death penalty. However, his personal feelings didn't enter into the decision. The people of Wyoming County had elected him to serve, and Jerry represented them. The death penalty was one issue a majority of county residents were in favor of, and he believed it was his responsibility in the end to pursue it in the despicable murder of a child. The circumstantial basis of the case and whether Rachel would be prosecuted were sticking points for him during those long months of indecision. Nothing could be left to chance in such a significant trial. Because of the high stakes in a death penalty case, the state provided other resources for prosecutors beyond Diane and Harry.

From the time the death penalty legislation was passed, a section was included to establish New York Prosecutors Training Institute (NYPTI). Seminars were scheduled to train attorneys for death-penalty cases. Jerry had attended its top-shelf workshop, which had brought in the best death-penalty litigation attorneys from around the United States. The executive director of the Institute had traveled from Albany to meet with Jerry soon after the possibility of a death penalty case arose. He provided assistance for the DA's office in answering the tower of motions from the defense arguing about the constitutionality of the death penalty. Diane recalled that after a few of these death-penalty cases had been tried, defense motions tended to be pro forma, which was advantageous to the prosecution in responding to them. Although it didn't happen in the Zaldivar case, she remembered a case she had assisted on where a defense attorney who had taken a computer disk with the motions had forgotten to change the name to the correct defendant when he filed them.

Because of the number of motions and their length—some hundreds of pages were distributed between the Public Defender and DA—floppy disks were used, which was new for both offices. However, the motions and technology paled in significance for Jerry and Diane. The paperwork and how it was communicated between the attorneys was no big deal.

"The big deal," Jerry said "was that Angel Colon murdered Samantha Zaldivar and buried her in a farmer's field. That was a big deal. What Steve was doing was a big deal. We were more concerned about the evidence and how we were going to convict this guy."

Just as for the previous year, the number of investigations continued to mount in the first quarter of the year. The first two weeks of January, I investigated an apartment fire in Warsaw and a horrific pedestrian fatality in the Town of Orangeville on January 13. The next day, I was once again at the Monroe County Medical Examiner's office to witness the autopsy of the victim. Later in the month, I was called in to assist social services with the forensic work on a child abuse case. These were just the tip of the iceberg for investigators that month.

The heavy workload continued uninterrupted into February with more investigation required on the December arson fire in the Village of Perry and several meetings with the FBI in Buffalo leading up to the one-year anniversary of Samantha's disappearance. The community still mourned, and it was a time of reflection for everyone. Local residents purchased a tangible memorial to Samantha, a granite marker placed behind the dugout at the Wethersfield Little League diamond, just across the road from where her body was found. The memory of the hundreds of people who walked the fields shoulder to shoulder and the landfill search immediately came to my mind, along with the memory of the night we took her from the shallow grave. My job wasn't done yet, and every spare minute was spent on the never-ending task of cataloging and cross-referencing every piece of evidence.

March 1998

Shovels were processed with the help of Captain Michael Melton of the Amherst Police Department at the beginning of March. An extensive forensic examination for latent fingerprints was conducted.

A call from the Perry PD came in, requesting my help with a forensic examination in a rape investigation, and three days later, I was sifting through the ashes of a house fire in the Village of Wyoming. Constant vigilance and organization were necessary to keep all these different cases' evidence straight and accessible.

Mid-March, I was called out for the investigation of an unattended death. A person who dies and isn't found for perhaps days or longer is classified as an unattended death. It can happen when someone doesn't have family or friends around to check on them, or it can be a suicide. The deceased had been transported to Bertrand Chaffee Memorial Hospital in Springville, New York. The following day, I was present for the autopsy, which was performed at the Erie County Medical Examiner's Office in Buffalo.

Friday, March 20, 1998

My day began with a follow-up on the rape investigation in the Village of Perry.

Later in the afternoon, I was called out to investigate and process the scene where a man's body had been found alongside a country road in the Town of Bennington, which borders Erie County. The body was in a ditch approximately five feet off the shoulder of the roadway. The victim, a Caucasian male, was lying on his back on some broken branches from a previous ice storm. Snow was all around the body when first responders arrived. There were no signs of any fresh footprints along the shoulder. The dirt road was extremely muddy, and there were no fresh tire impressions except for the first responders. Investigators worked into the evening attempting to identify the victim as there was no identification found or any vehicle in the area. After I processed the crime scene, the body was secured and the hands were bagged and sealed with evidence tape. It was then removed and transported to the Monroe County Medical Examiner's office by Wyoming County Coroner Rene Hill and Jack Marsh from a local funeral home.

Saturday, March 21, 1998

Weekend duty began at 7:30 AM, and I was back on the road to the Monroe County Medical Examiner's Office to attend the autopsy of the victim found in Bennington. The medical examiner determined as we already suspected that the man had been murdered. The preliminary finding of the cause of death was head injuries caused by a blunt object. The skull was fractured, and it appeared that the victim had been struck with some type of a rigid item. While at the medical examiner's office, I received a call from Undersheriff Ely that contact had been made with the victim's mother, and she would meet with me at the medical examiner's office at 2:00 PM. At 2:45 PM, she identified her son, and investigators scrambled to create a timeline, starting to interview as many relatives and friends as they could.

Tuesday, March 24 – Tuesday, March 31, 1998

The WCSO investigative team had another homicide to investigate, and it was providential that Harry Frank was available. Early on, we determined that the body had been dumped in Wyoming County, and most likely, the homicide had occurred in Erie County. But we needed to be 100 percent sure that in fact the crime had been committed outside of our county. We continued our investigation in the City of Buffalo, interviewing people connected with the victim. Investigator Harry Frank paved the way for us to see the right people in the Homicide Division of the Buffalo PD.

The vehicle belonging to the victim was located, so on March 23, 1998, I made the trip to the Buffalo Police Department's Seneca Street Garage to process the car. Due to the amount of snow still on the vehicle, I took some initial photographs and planned to come back at a later date. Then it was off to the Monroe County Medical Examiner's office to pick up evidence from the autopsy and transport it to the Monroe County Crime Laboratory. On March 26, 1998, Investigator Davis and I made a return trip to the Seneca Street Police Garage and worked on processing the vehicle for the next five hours or so.

Then Davis and I worked into the night, conducting additional interviews with the victim's friends in the city of Buffalo. For the next two weeks, investigators were saturating the City of Buffalo and surrounding areas, conducting more than 100 interviews along with investigators from the Buffalo Police Department. With the Zaldivar case intensifying and enough evidence uncovered to show that this crime hadn't occurred in Wyoming County, WCSO investigators met on April 6, 1998 with Investigators Kenneth Black, Paul Jackson, Joseph Debergalis, James Probst, and Henry Haas from the New York State Police. Investigators Harry Frank, Dave Davis, and I were assigned to meet with NYSP investigators and advise them of the status of the case. This took several hours, and then we drove out to the scene where the body had been recovered. From there, we all went to the NYSP Clarence sub-station for more discussion.

Shortly thereafter, investigators spread out and were hitting the streets to attempt additional interviews. This was a welcome event as we were being stretched to the limits, and new leads were constantly coming in on the case. Davis and I were very familiar with several of these investigators from the NYSP and had worked together on many previous cases, which made this transition easy. It was a relief to hand off the role of lead agency at this point and just assist the state police.

April 1998

On April 8, a day before the deadline to file, Jerry did submit the death penalty paperwork with the Wyoming County Court Clerk. He called LaVallee, who was in Albany, to let her know she needed to make a trip to Warsaw for this news. Jerry stood outside the Wyoming County Courthouse with a swarm of reporters, TV cameras, and photographers surrounding him. While a bouquet of microphones stood on stands before him, he told the media, "I took a lot of time, talked to a lot of people, and did a lot of soul searching."

The defense team had sixty days to file any other motions now that the death penalty would be sought. Colon's attorneys reiterated that it was a circumstantial case and not appropriate for the death penalty. They warned it would only delay closure for the victim's family, and they were ready to fight it out in the courtroom. Law enforcement supported Jerry's decision all the way. I believed the evidence would definitely prove Colon was guilty without reasonable doubt. The trial wasn't expected to happen until later in 1999—over a year away.

Bruno Stra stood on the edge of the crowd, nodding his approval and telling reporters he was happy that the case was finally going forward and they would find out the truth for the sake of his granddaughter. Even if Jerry hadn't filed for the death penalty, Bruno would have trusted the DA's judgment about the case.

I didn't have much time to think about the decision, because on April 9, I was working at the Buffalo PD's office on the case of murder victim who had been dumped in Bennington. We were making progress on the case, thanks to Harry Frank, who accompanied me to Buffalo to meet with both the FBI and Buffalo City Police for the entire day. He knew the right contacts and opened doors that made the investigation run smoother.

CHAPTER 20

May – July 1998

The prosecution and defense teams sat down with Judge Mark Dadd to talk about the logistical issues of the case, which were staggering to consider. They gathered in the judge's chambers, hoping to come to some conclusions. The amount of evidence was of vital concern.

The lawyers and judge were also concerned about how many days before jury selection the evidence should be marked as exhibits for trial. Keeping track of it all would be a challenge as well. The trial was expected to be lengthy. Then there was jury selection itself. The courthouse wasn't capable of handling the large number of jurors that were expected to be called during the voir dire portion of the trial. Judge Dadd estimated that they might need to call as many as 1,500 individuals divided up over a number of days because each would have to be "death-qualified" to be eligible to be part of the jury pool. It would be a challenge to select a jury. A "death-qualified" juror must not be in opposition to imposing the death penalty, but also must be willing to impose a life sentence in prison for the capital murder.

The group began discussing use of the North Java Fire Hall as the place to have potential jurors appear since it was the largest facility in the county. Part of the problem was that the courthouse was under construction and major renovation. Parking around the courthouse was a nightmare and couldn't accommodate the anticipated crowd. The jury selection process could take up to six weeks, and the trial might last two months or more. This case would also put the legal system to the test in our small county.

Representatives from each side and Judge Dadd took a trip out to North Java to look it over with Undersheriff Ely. A short-term lease was discussed with the fire department because of the length of time needed for the proceedings. Research began on what was necessary to hold court proceedings at a different location than the county courthouse. The judge thought a motion before the New York Supreme Court would be necessary to use the North Java facility. Yet more paperwork.

While every spare moment the investigative team had was spent in preparing the evidence for trial, the steady stream of new cases never faltered with more fires, motor vehicle accidents, unattended deaths, attendance at autopsies, trips to the crime lab, and meetings with the DA's office. Conversations about charging Rachel were cropping up, and Jerry and Diane began exploring that option. Angel Colon remained silent, and his attorneys affirmed his innocence. Felony charges were on the table for Rachel—first-degree hindering prosecution and first-degree tampering with evidence. They began preparing the paperwork for the grand jury that would meet in July.

The fatigue and stress of managing so many cases was exacting its toll on the department. Days off were cancelled unless they were essential, overtime was expected, and everyone—dispatchers, deputies, investigators, correction officers—everyone at the sheriff's department did their best to put the job first. Families and any kind of social life were running way behind in our priorities, which is always the norm for law enforcement, but this timeframe proved to be the most intense that I had ever experienced. Even my membership in the Perry Rotary Club proved to be more difficult because of the organization's weekly meetings. If I didn't make the Perry meeting, attendance at another club in the area was required. It was a constant juggling act.

Sheriff Capwell remembers the total dedication to the work to resolve cases, which he believes shows the outstanding commitment of the department.

"We had a great bunch of people, and they took care of things," he recalled, looking back at 1997 and 1998.

Physically, my body was way more exhausted than I imagined, and on July 1, I received the message loud and clear. Bent over my desk, I was writing on the legal pad that contained the evidence information I was readying for Colon's trial. The last thing I remember was getting up and walking toward Deputy Dan Hummel. It was a good thing he was there at the time. I passed out mid-stride and collapsed on the floor. Dan took charge and got me transported to the hospital. High blood pressure, dehydration, and not eating properly landed me in a timeout from work for several weeks. The doctor adjusted my medication and ordered mandatory rest at home. A month off proved to be good medicine, and I returned to duty on August 3, although I would have preferred an earlier date.

Tuesday, July 21, 1998

While I was at home recuperating, the case carried on, and Jerry went to the grand jury with his two charges against Rachel. The defense counsel called them "cryptic" and "meritless," but the grand jury handed down an indictment on both hindering prosecution and tampering with evidence. She was charged with Class D and E felonies. The indictment read: "rendered criminal assistance to Angel Colon, a person who had committed a Class A felony, to wit: murder, knowing or believing that Angel Colon had engaged in conduct constituting a Class A felony to wit: murder."

Sergeant Ed Till took her into custody quietly, snapping the cuffs on her hands which were behind her back. He then assisted her into the back of the sheriff's car. Late in the afternoon, standing with her attorneys, David Saleh and Anthony Irrera, she was arraigned before Judge Dadd, who set bail at $100,000. If convicted, she could face seven years in prison. Bruno watched his daughter go through the court process and then be escorted out of the courtroom by deputies. He was having a hard time with the DA's decision to go after her.

Without the means to post bail, she was remanded to the county jail. The distraught father and grandfather told reporters that he didn't understand why the prosecutors had waited such a long time to bring the charges and pledged to stand by her. He still couldn't understand why she continued to support Colon.

The case once again took a physical toll that day when Jerry collapsed at home and was taken to the Wyoming County Community Hospital. Blood pressure medication issues were blamed, and doctors kept him there until Friday. He remained at home for another week before taking up his responsibilities again.

Friday, July 24, 1998

The sheriff's department transported both Angel and Rachel for an appearance in Wyoming County Family Court. A deputy on each side escorted them into the courthouse. They took their places at the tables with their attorneys. Angela and Cassandra were the subjects of the hearing. With both parents in jail, temporary custody had to go to someone.

Carmen Guzman, Angel's mother, had been living with Rachel and the girls as they awaited his trial. Now it looked like she would be granted temporary custody to care for the two girls. The DSS and girls' guardian ad litem, an attorney appointed to represent the girls, were agreeable about the arrangement, but there were many hoops for Guzman to jump through. The grandmother had to undergo a psychological exam and criminal background check. Cassandra had to remain in the Head Start program; both girls had to continue in counseling, and the counselor's recommendations had to be followed. Guzman agreed to all the conditions.

Rachel faced another charge of child neglect that coincided with her criminal charges. That petition was put off to a later date. Her bit of good news was supervised calls to her daughters would be permitted. Colon's attorney requested the same treatment, but the judge denied that request, reiterating that he was to have no contact with the two girls.

When the media approached Guzman outside the courtroom, she told them that eviction papers had been served on her and that she might have to find a new home. It wouldn't affect the custody arrangement, but different living arrangements had to be approved by the DSS prior to any move.

Guzman wasn't the only one interested in gaining custody of Angela and Cassandra. Two other grandmothers, Ruth Velarde, Rachel's mother, and Maria Padilla, Noel Zaldivar's mother, were seeking permanent custody. The family court situation continued to be complex.

Besides hearing the family court matter, Judge Dadd had October 26 as the date for jury selection to begin. Pressure on everyone increased, especially for Colon and Stra. We felt something had to happen before that date. Something had to give.

CHAPTER 21

Wednesday, August 12, 1998

Meetings between the prosecution and defense teams had been frequent and intense over the last week. The DA was talking about offering a plea deal that would allow Colon to admit to second-degree murder. This would take the death penalty off the table. Jerry remained unconvinced that a jury would convict the defendant of first-degree murder. Too much was circumstantial in his opinion. There were no eyewitnesses to the crime, to the burial, not even a positive ID as to the driver of the Bronco leaving the trailer court on the night Samantha was murdered. He was unsure of Dr. Smith's testimony because of his initial finding that the suffocation could have been accidental.

However, the defense had its own doubts. After additional training in New York City, including a mock trial, Public Defender Norm Effman was quite certain his client would receive the death penalty from a jury. He would welcome a lesser charge to keep his client from death row. In many ways, it appeared to be a legal standoff, but everyone wanted resolution to the case, not only for Samantha's family, but for the community, which had taken Samantha's murder personally.

There was every reason to believe Angel Colon was guilty. The weight of the forensic evidence was heavily against him. The pubic hairs found in her bedroom could not be excluded as his. Samantha could not be excluded as the source of the DNA obtained from the piece of foam in the bedroom or from the passenger seat of the truck upholstery fabric. Rachel, Noel, Angela, and Cassandra could be excluded as contributors of the DNA obtained from the evidence. The process of elimination through DNA evidence brought us directly to Angel Colon and Samantha Zaldivar. No one else. The neighbor had heard her scream around 8:30 PM, and another neighbor had seen the Bronco leave the trailer park in the middle of night. Her stomach contents attested to the school lunch being her last meal from that day. The first-grader had never gone out the door to the bus on Thursday. No one had kidnapped her. We knew something horrific had happened the night her mother had gone to class.

Rachel hadn't helped herself or her children throughout the investigation. Support of her boyfriend had everyone shaking their heads. Now with two felony counts against her and the likelihood of a conviction, she faced real prison time. She also had misdemeanor charges pending in the Village of Warsaw for lewd behavior in the county's parking lot. She'd allegedly exposed herself toward the windows of the jail after a visit to Colon the previous fall.

The specifics of the felony charges were that she had cut out the blood-soaked section of Samantha's mattress, thrown it out, and lied to investigators about why the piece of foam was missing. If convicted, her remaining daughters would be in the foster care system. Angel's mother had only temporary custody of the girls. There was no guarantee that she would get permanent custody or that the girls would remain together. The family would be even more fractured.

Colon wasn't amenable to pleading guilty to the lesser charge of second-degree murder—at first. The reality that his daughters and his fiancée were going to pay for his actions if he didn't break his silence finally changed his thinking. He was going to have to divulge the terrible secret of what had happened the night of February 25, 1997. Proud of his Puerto Rican heritage, the secret he'd kept was more than shameful to his culture. It was anathema, just as it is for American culture, and would damage his machismo. But pride, or maybe fear, kept him from admitting his crime. It was something he wouldn't state in public—before a judge or anyone. The attorneys kept working at hammering out an acceptable plea agreement.

Finally, after a marathon session on Wednesday between the lawyers, along with a meeting of several hours between just Rachel and Angel, the deal was made. Rachel learned from her boyfriend that he had killed her daughter. She alternated between anger and tears. The meeting was the tipping point.

There were a lot of conditions, each one carefully considered by both sides. Colon would plead guilty to second-degree murder with depraved indifference to human life if the other charges against him were dropped, including the sexual abuse charges. He admitted to killing Samantha, to cutting out the piece of mattress and disposing of it, and of transporting her body to Frank Conrad's field, burying her in the middle of the night. Because he admitted to cutting out the piece of mattress, Rachel's charges would be lowered to a misdemeanor charge of hindering prosecution, because she lied about the mattress to protect Colon.

There was also another twist in the case. Both Colon and Stra would plead guilty to the agreed-upon charges using a proffer. Most often in a plea agreement, the defendant tells the judge what he or she did in open court. This wouldn't be the case. A written statement—the proffer—would be given. It was a confession by paper essentially. Judge Dadd would accept it.

Both waived their right to appeal, bringing closure to the case. Appeals if Colon was convicted of first-degree murder and given the death penalty could go on for a decade. Rachel would receive a sentence of time served and a one-year conditional discharge. Unless she was arrested in the next twelve months, she was a free woman. Colon would serve a mandatory twenty-five years before any eligibility of parole.

I vividly remember the call I received from Jerry Stout that day. After nine months of preparation, he told me to stop organizing the evidence because Colon was taking a plea. I was at my desk with a yellow pad and pen actually working on the cataloging of the evidence when the call came in. After our conversation, I sat motionless for several minutes, stunned at the news. My mind swirled around, trying to absorb what I had just heard. There would be no trial—it was unbelievable. I just stared at the handwritten list of items on the paper. The months of investigation and trial preparation were over. Although it was hard to process, there was also great relief.

CHAPTER 22

Thursday, August 13, 1998

Colon was in handcuffs, dressed in a gray shirt and black pants, and Rachel wore a print dress. As part of the security detail, I had to help negotiate them safely to the courtroom and back. Media was everywhere, as were family members and interested citizens. The courthouse was packed again. This was the day the pair would plead guilty to the agreed-upon charges. Rachel was emotional and nervous while Colon remained impassive.

The court proceedings went smoothly with the withdrawal of the notice of intent to seek the death penalty from the DA. Colon calmly answered the judge's questions with "yes" and "no" as he stood before him.

The factual proffer didn't provide details about how he'd injured Samantha, but he admitted to the crime. He also didn't say what he'd done with Samantha's backpack or where he'd disposed of the bloody piece of mattress. An excerpt from the proffer:

I was alone with Samantha in her room around 8:30 PM. I had no intent of hurting her. I unintentionally injured her. She was bleeding, and she was crying out. I was trying to help her, to calm her down, and I put the pillow over her face to quiet her down.

... The next thing I knew she was not breathing. I panicked. ... My mind was spinning. I decided I would not tell

anyone. When Rachel got home, I made sure she did not go into Samantha's room by telling her Samantha was asleep.

... Later that night while Rachel was asleep, I cleaned up the blood in the bedroom, dressed Samantha's body, removed the evidence and Samantha's body from the trailer. I placed Samantha's body in the Bronco and drove it to a field about 300 yards from the trailer where I buried her in a shallow grave. I also decided that I would say Samantha was alive on the following morning and that I saw her leave the trailer for the school bus about 7:18 AM.

Rachel never knew what happened that night. When she and I told the police about her going to bed and her not seeing Samantha that night and the next morning, that was the truth. Rachel had nothing to do with Samantha's death and she did not know that I did either. I know that she said that she had earlier cut the mattress because one of the kids had wet the bed. That is not true. I cut the mattress that night because Samantha had bled on it.

He admitted to depraved indifference to human life, which aligned with second-degree murder. His sentencing was set for August 26.

Rachel cried throughout her time before the judge, answering "yes" and "no" to his questions while leaning on the desk. Rachel's proffer went as follows:

During the course of the investigation of Angel Colon, I lied to law enforcement agents when they questioned me about the hole in Samantha's mattress. I told them that I had cut the mattress earlier because one of the kids had wet the bed. That statement was not true. I never cut the mattress.

I made these statements to law enforcement agents to provide assistance to Angel and deceive the agents and prevent them from lodging criminal charges against Angel. I now understand Angel has admitted to committing a felony.

Emotions erupted from family and community members when it was over. Rachel was processed out of the jail—free to be with her daughters and Carmen Guzman, who were now living in LeRoy, NY. Her sentencing was scheduled for October 1, and the conditional discharge was in satisfaction of all charges pending against her. Angel was led out to a patrol car by Undersheriff Ely to go back to the jail. Microphones followed both legal teams to get their comments.

The defense and prosecution were satisfied with the outcome. Samantha's murderer would go to prison for at least twenty-five years. The defense team had saved their client from facing the death penalty, and he'd owned up to what he'd done. The family and community had closure. Defense counsel Norm Effman and Undersheriff Ely, along with DA Stout and Special ADA LaVallee, urged the community to begin the healing process. LaVallee said that Colon's conviction was a "homerun" for this type of case.

Bruno was relieved for his daughter and glad to see Colon finally admit to killing his granddaughter. He'd suspected Colon all along. Colon's prison sentence would satisfy him, and he would continue to help Rachel. Lucely Zaldivar was contacted by the press for her reaction, which was anger over the removal of the death penalty and how Rachel walked away. Samantha's father Noel was also stunned by the sudden plea agreement.

Those who knew the family had mixed opinions, but most were glad to see resolution to the case. However, they felt Rachel had gotten off with a slap on the hand. Many Wyoming County residents felt the same about Samantha's mother, but Diane LaVallee told reporters that once Colon admitted to cutting the mattress, there really wasn't another charge they could prove in a trial. The evidence just wasn't there.

Elaine Rowe, owner of Rowe's General Store in Hermitage, and her employees were shocked, as were residents of the trailer park that it was over. They had helped with the search, supported the family, and shed tears the night Samantha's body was found. Emotions were still raw, and the news was difficult to process.

Tuesday, August 18 – Friday, August 21, 1998

Even though the final step in the justice system was Colon's formal sentencing, there were still tasks for me connected to the case. I dropped off the completed photograph files, which had the evidence photos from day one of the investigation, to DA Stout and Public Defender Norm Effman.

On Thursday, August 20, I left Warsaw for Albany to pick up all the remaining evidence that was at the New York State Police Crime Lab. It was a surreal trip driving on the NYS Thruway to Albany. It would be the last one on this case. The 263-mile one-way trip didn't seem long at all either way. I returned to Warsaw on Friday to secure the evidence and begin the process of boxing everything up for storage. The heavy responsibilities of the case were now over. Law enforcement had done their job of gathering evidence to build a solid case for the DA, and we'd had some providential help in discovering Samantha's body. The justice system had done its job as well. Samantha's killer was going to prison.

Wednesday, August 26, 1998

Angel Colon stood before Judge Mark Dadd and heard his sentence of twenty-five years to life—no appeals—and no parole opportunities for at least twenty-five years. He would be remanded to the custody of the New York State Department of Corrections. His incarceration would be at a men's maximum security facility, and he would undergo an evaluation before being sent to one. The intake of a new inmate could take up to six weeks, and the process included the DOC looking at the type of crime committed and the level of risk.

The courtroom was once again overflowing. TV crews were ready with cameras outside, reporters and microphones, all poised to capture the reactions of the family and lawyers. Maria Padilla and her daughter Lucely Zaldivar were present along with Lucely's sixteen-year-old daughter. They were outraged at Colon's seemingly light sentence. Lucely voiced her displeasure in the courtroom and outside of it with the media. Rachel Stra was conspicuous by her absence, and it seemed no one knew why she didn't attend, not even her attorney David Saleh.

For those who believed that the case should have been tried and Colon given the death penalty, that victory would have been short-lived. On June 24, 2004, New York State's Supreme Court ruled that the death penalty violated the state constitution. Later on in 2008, death-row was eliminated by then Governor David Paterson. Along with the exorbitant trial costs, there would have been the expense of multiple appeals for years, and Colon would never have been executed.

The investigative team that was present avoided the media circus and went back to the sheriff's office and started talking. We went back over details of the case, reminiscing about the months of work we'd accomplished together. Harry Frank, the special investigator, joined us that day as well. There was a strange feeling in the room, as if none of us wanted to leave each other's company. We were thankful that the case was over, but the intensity of the moment and what all of us had been through to arrive at this point was emotional. After about a half an hour, we decided to get some lunch from a nearby restaurant. Strangely enough, the Capital Defenders Team was having lunch at one of the tables when we walked in. We went over to talk with them, and they told us, "Good job, guys." Their look of relief matched ours.

EPILOGUE

The first thing I must say is that my heart goes out to the families of Samantha Zaldivar, Angel Colon, and Rachel Stra. We know law enforcement and the community suffered, but one can only imagine what these families went through. My thoughts and prayers continue even after twenty years.

During the investigation and after it was settled, I continued to hear rumors and stories about this case that were not true. I would be out and about and hear people talking about the Zaldivar case without realizing who I was. It was truly amazing and often troubling to hear some of the comments. Sometimes the remarks were negative about the sheriff's office and members of the families associated with this case. I felt strongly that this story needed to be told as the general public really didn't know the details of the investigation. There were members of our own department who didn't know all the facts. The investigators on the team were the only ones who had access to reports in confidential files and not the whole department. It was very important throughout the entire investigation to keep leaks to a minimum. I thought some day after I retired I would attempt to write a book about this tragic story.

As time went by, I thought about this project and kept putting it off for another year. Several years ago, I read about Laurinda Wallace, an author who used to live in Wyoming County and actually worked for a law firm behind the Wyoming County Courthouse. We had known each other during our careers and worked together on a variety of issues that had crossed our paths. I reached out to her and advised her of what I wanted to do concerning this book. Laurinda was very interested as she has written numerous novels with an investigation and murder-mystery theme. She was excited as much as I was to go ahead, and we started the project.

After several years of research, reading through thousands of pages of documents, and conducting interviews with people involved in the case, we began this very difficult journey. Collaborating with Laurinda was enjoyable, and I felt fortunate to be working on this project with her.

Being retired from the WCSO since 2002, there hasn't been a day that I don't think about Samantha. This was probably the biggest case that ever occurred in Wyoming County and certainly during my time at the WCSO. This tragedy drew the community and law enforcement together like no one could have ever imagined. It's no secret that sometimes different law enforcement agencies have difficulty working together on cases. I'm proud to say that wasn't the situation here, as egos were left at the door. Everyone had the same goal, and that was to fight for Samantha and bring this case to a successful conclusion. I can't say enough about the FBI, New York State Police, Amherst Police Department, Batavia Police Department, Buffalo Police Department, New York State Department of Environmental Conservation, Erie County Sheriff's Department, Niagara County Sheriff's Department, Genesee County Sheriff's Department, Livingston County Sheriff's Department, Monroe County Sheriff's Department Rochester, NY, and the Monroe County Sheriff's Department in Key West, Florida. The members of these departments outside of Wyoming County were true professionals, and many were experts in their field.

I must say thanks to all of the agencies in Wyoming County and the police departments in Arcade, Attica, Perry, and Warsaw Police Departments, which I worked with daily. And thanks must go to all of the employees of the Wyoming

County Sheriff's Department. All of us were constantly asked to go above and beyond during this time. Our dispatchers were tested as they took on additional responsibilities to assist the investigators. Looking back, the caseload was truly overwhelming, but the exceptional effort that everyone put forward got us through that tough time. The residents of Wyoming County should be commended for their outpouring of support throughout the entire investigation.

This book is about what I observed throughout the investigation. The complex investigation could not have survived without the guidance of many qualified personnel who stepped up to the plate: the Wyoming County District Attorney's Office under the direction of District Attorney Gerald L. Stout, ADA David DiMatteo, ADA Mike Kelly, ADA Keith Kibler, ADA Tim Moran, ADA Len Opanashuk and ADA Toby Rey; Wyoming County Judges Mark Dadd and Michael Griffith; Ms. Diane LaVallee and Special Investigator Harry Frank from the New York State Attorney General's Office; and former New York State Attorney General Dennis Vacco. The expertise of the Monroe County Crime Laboratory and Medical Examiner's Office, especially Dr. Thomas Smith and Dr. Beno, along with Dr. Baden from the New York State Police Crime Laboratory, were vital to this case's successful conclusion. A special thanks to my family for all of the sacrifices over the years.

I know I have not listed everyone, and I apologize. It is my hope this book brings a better understanding of what occurred and the effects it had on the whole community. Again our thoughts and prayers are with Samantha as she will never be forgotten.

More about Stephen C. Tarbell

Born in Rochester, New York, Stephen relocated to Perry, New York in 1970. After earning a Criminal Justice degree from Genesee Community College, Batavia, NY in 1978, he went to work for the Wyoming County Sheriff's Department. Over a twenty-three-year career, he served as a deputy sheriff, scientific evidence technician, technical sergeant, and an investigator specializing in crime scene and fire investigations. He also was a private fire investigator working for many years after retirement.

While working for the sheriff's department, Steve went on to earn a BS in Criminal Justice/Public Administration/Accounting from Empire State SUNY College and a Master's degree from the Nelson A. Rockefeller School of Criminal Justice at the University of Albany, NY. He is also a graduate of the Dennis A. Pelletier Institute of County Government, Cornell University.

Steve has worn many hats in public service, including: a member on the Warsaw Central School Board of Education, Wyoming County Youth Court Coordinator, Deputy Mayor of the Village of Silver Springs, Town Councilman and Supervisor for the Town of Castile, and board member for the Wyoming County Board of Supervisors and the Wyoming County Community Hospital Board of Managers.

He has received numerous awards, including Wyoming County Deputy of the Year and the department's Commendation award, the Eastman Kodak Law Enforcement Photography award, and the Leadership Wyoming Alumni Award. He was inducted in 2014 to the Genesee Community College Hall of Fame. He received a U.S. Department of Justice, Federal Bureau of Investigation Commendation for the Samantha Zaldivar investigation.

He and his wife Pam have a son and daughter, who are both graduates of Letchworth Central School, where Pam was an elementary teacher at Letchworth Central for many years. Steve and Pam enjoy spending time with their grandchildren now that they are both retired. Steve is a member of the St. Regis Indian Reservation, Mohawk Tribe, Akwesasne, New York and is proud of his heritage.

More about Laurinda L. Wallace

Born in Castile, New York, Laurinda was a lifelong resident of Wyoming County until 2003 when she and her husband David moved to the high desert of Arizona.

She earned a paralegal certificate from Southern Career Institute in 1991 and is a 2001 graduate of Houghton College, NY with a BS in Management.

Much of her career was spent as a paralegal at a Warsaw, NY law firm and in administration at Houghton College. Laurinda served the community as a trustee for the C.A. Greene Library in Castile for over a decade. Most of her tenure was spent as the Secretary/Treasurer. She was active in the Project Read program and fundraising activities for the library.

Since moving to Arizona, Laurinda has worked in criminal law at the Cochise County Legal Defender's Office and recently retired from the Palominas School District. She now writes full-time and loves spending time with her grandsons as often as possible.

She has been published in several print magazines, including *Guideposts* and has been a contributor to a number of online publications since 2005. She is the author of the Gracie Andersen mystery series which is set in Wyoming County, and two other inspirational titles. Laurinda is the recipient of multiple Poets and Writers grants and *Washed Up*, the fourth Gracie Andersen mystery, was a semifinalist in the 2016 Kindle Book awards in the mystery category.

Laurinda is a member of Sisters in Crime, a national organization for women mystery writers, and the Tucson, Arizona chapter of Sisters in Crime. She writes two popular blogs, SimplyLife and The Business of Writing. For more information, visit: http://laurindawallace.com.

NOTES

Chapter 1

1. Linder, D. WCSO report. 26 February 1997.

2. Eck, G. WCSO report. 26 February 1997.

3. Spink, D. WCSO report. 26 February 1997.

4. Stra, R. interview by WCSO. 26 February 1997.

5. WCSO missing juvenile incident report.26 February 1997.

Chapter 2

1. Eck, G. WCSO report. 26 February 1997.

2. Spink, D. WCSO report. 26 February 1997, 27 February 1997.

3. Neighbors, interviews by WCSO. Various dates February/March 1997.

4. Tarbell, S. WCSO report. 26 February 1997.

5. Colon, A. interview by WCSO. 26 February 1997.

Chapter 3

1. Paul Mrozek. "Searchers look for missing girl." *The Daily News,* 27 February 1997.

2. Miller, S. WCSO report. 26 February 1997.

3. Tarbell, S. WCSO report. 27 February 1997.

4. Letchworth Central School personnel statements. Various dates February 1997.

5. FBI/WCSO meeting notes. 4 March 1997.

6. Crino, T. interview by S.C. Tarbell and L.L. Wallace 1 February 2017.

7. Velarde, R. interview by FBI. 17 March 1997.

8. Suarez, A. interview by FBI.18 March 1997.

9. DiMatteo, D. interview by S.C. Tarbell and L.L. Wallace 25 April 2017.

10. FBI Search Report. 27 February 1997.

Chapter 4

1. Stra, R. interviews by FBI. 27 February 1997, 28 February 1997.

2. Zaldivar, N. interview by FBI. 28 February 1997.

3. Wyoming Co. homemaker aide, interview by FBI. 28 February 1997.

4. Johnson, L. interview by S.C. Tarbell 9 November 2016.

5. FBI statement by L. Johnson. 28 February 1997.

6. Spink, D. WCSO report. 28 February 1997.

Chapter 5

1. Trevitt, A., Trevitt, M.*, interviews by FBI. 3 March 1997, 5 March 1997

2. Tarbell, S. WCSO evidence report. 1 March 1997.

3. Raymond Coniglio. "Hermitage search effort scaled back." *The Daily News,* 1 March 1997.

Chapter 6

1. Fuller, A. interviews by FBI/WCSO.

2. Zaldivar, L. interview by FBI. 3 March 1997

3. Tarbell, S. WCSO evidence report. 2-3 March 1997

4. Johnson, L. interview by S.C. Tarbell. 9 November 2016.

5. Spink, D. WCSO report. 2-3 March 1997

6. Trevitt, M.*, interview by FBI. 3 March 1997

Chapter 7

1. Spink, D. WCSO report. 4 March 1997.

2. Tarbell, S. WCSO evidence report. 4 March 1997.

3. Stout G./LaVallee, D. interview by S.C. Tarbell and L.L. Wallace 7 December 2016.

4. Spink, D. Interview by S.C. Tarbell 6 December 2016.

5. Eck, G. interview by S.C. Tarbell 1 November 2016.

6. Raymond Coniglio. "Colon faces obstruction charges." *The Daily News,* 5 March 1997.

7. Stra, R. interview by FBI. 4 March 1997.

Chapter 8

1. Raymond Coniglio. "Investigators search septic tank." *The Daily News*, 6 March 1997 and 7 March 1997.

2. Tarbell, S. WCSO Evidence report. 5 March 1997 and 6 March 1997.

3. Dunn, D. interview by FBI 6 March 1997.

4. Rodriguez, A. interview by FBI 5 March 1997.

Chapter 9

1. Tarbell, S. WCSO evidence report. 7 March 1997 and 8 March 1997.

2. Paul Mrozek. "High-tech equipment to aid in search." *The Daily News,* 7 March 1997.

3. Paul Mrozek. "Police pursue leads." *The Daily News*, 10 March 1997.

4. O'Connor, T. interview by FBI. 7 March 1997.

5. Spink, D., WCSO report. 7 March 1997 and 8 March 1997.

6. J. Shearing, interview by FBI. 7 March 1997.

7. Search plan reports. WCSO and other agencies. Various dates.

Chapter 10

1. Raymond Coniglio. "Stra's children still not returned." *The Daily News*, 12 March 1997.

2. Eck, G. WCSO report. 11 March 1997.

3. Tarbell, S. WCSO evidence report. 11 March 1997.

4. Johnson, L. interview by S.C. Tarbell 9 November 2016.

5. Spink, D.WCSO report. 11 March 1997.

Chapter 11

1. Paul Mrozek. "Crisis team in place at girl's school." *The Daily News*, 14 March 1997.

2. Raymond Coniglio. "Stra gets her daughters back." *The Daily News*, 15 March 1997.

2. Tarbell, S. WCSO evidence report. 14 March 1997.

3. Monroe County Crime Lab reports. Various dates.

4. Tarbell, S. WCSO daybook.

Chapter 12

1. Tarbell, S. WCSO evidence report.

2. WCSO timeline 16 March 1997-19 April 1997.

3. WCSO luminol test report. 21 March 1997.

4. Monroe County Crime Lab reports. Various dates.

Chapter 13

1. Smith, M. interview by S.C. Tarbell and L.L. Wallace. 3 February 2017.

2. WCSO Zaldivar search documents. Various dates.

3. Tarbell, S. WCSO evidence report. Various dates in April 1997.

4. *The Daily News*, 21 March 1997 and 24 March 1997.

5. Monroe County Crime Lab reports. Various dates.

6. NYSP crime lab reports.

Chapter 14

1. Tarbell, S. WCSO evidence autopsy report. 23 May 1997-17 November 1997.

2. Tarbell, S. Body recovery report.

3. Tarbell, S. Body recovery report #2.

4. Tarbell, S. Body recovery addendum #3.

4. Capwell, A. interview by S.C. Tarbell and L.L. Wallace. 19 January 2017.

5. Smith, M. interview by S.C. Tarbell and L.L. Wallace. 3 February 2017.

6. Crino, T. interview by S.C. Tarbell and L.L. Wallace. 1 February 2017.

Chapter 15

1. Tarbell, S. WCSO evidence autopsy report 23 May 1997 -17 November 1997.

2. Tarbell, S. Beans and menu report.

3. Newspaper articles file #18.

4. Stout, G./LaVallee, D. interview by S.C. Tarbell and L.L. Wallace. 7 December 2016.

5. *The Daily News*, 29 May 1997.

6. Smith, M. interview by S.C. Tarbell and L.L. Wallace. 3 February 2017.

7. Monroe County medical examiner's report (quotes).

8. Tarbell, S. WCSO daybook.

Chapter 16

1. Tarbell, S. WCSO handwritten interview notes. 13 June 1997.

2. Lopez, L. statement. 18 June 1997.

3. Zaldivar, L. statement. 19 June 1997.

4. Zaldivar, N. statement. 19 June 1997.

5. Velarde, R statement. 20 June 1997.

6. Misc. handwritten interview notes. 21 June 1997.

7. Stout, G. /LaVallee, D. interview by S.C. Tarbell and L.L. Wallace. 7 December 2016.

Chapter 17

1. Eck, G. interview by S.C. Tarbell. 1 November 2016.

2. "Colon returns for arraignment," *Buffalo News*, 9 September1997.

3. "Colon won't fight return to NY," *The Daily News*, 9 August 1997.

4. "Vacco's office to assist Colon prosecution," *Buffalo News*, 19 August1997.

5. Stout, G./LaVallee, D. interview by S.C. Tarbell and L.L. Wallace. 7 December 2016.

6. CVs: G. Stout, D. LaVallee, N. Effman.

7. *Buffalo Evening News*, 25 July 1997.

8. "Colon may return by Sept. 2," *The Daily News*, 12 August 1997.

9. "Special Prosecutor Appointed," *The Daily News*, 19 August 1997.

Chapter 18

1. Tarbell, S. WCSO daybook.

2. Stout, G./LaVallee, D. interview by S.C. Tarbell and L.L. Wallace. 7 December 2016.

3. *The Daily News*, 10 September 1997.

4. Frank, H. interview with S.C. Tarbell and L.L. Wallace. 23 January 2017.

5. *The Daily News*, 17 September 1997. (Johnson Docs)

6. Tarbell, S. Evidence autopsy report.

Chapter 19

1. Tarbell, S. WCSO daybook.

2. Stout, G./LaVallee, D. interview by S.C. Tarbell and L.L. Wallace. 7 December 2016.

3. Paul Mrozek. "I did a lot of soul searching." *The Daily News*, 9 April 1998.

4. Re-interview of Fuller, A. by WCSO. 2 January 1998.

Chapter 20

1. Dadd, M. interview by S.C. Tarbell and L.L. Wallace 23 February 2017.

2. Stout, G./LaVallee, D. interview by S.C. Tarbell and L.L. Wallace. 7 December 2016.

3. Stra indictment.

4. Paul Mrozek. "Samantha's mother indicted." *The Daily News*, 22 July 1998.

5. Skip Tillinghast. "Stra indicted in Samantha case." *Country Courier*, 23 July 1998.

Chapter 21

1. Effman, N. interview by L.L. Wallace. 5 October 2016.

2. Stout, G. /LaVallee, D. interview by S.C. Tarbell and L.L. Wallace. 7 December 2016.

3. Paul Mrozek. "Officials call for healing to begin." *The Daily News*, 14 August 1998.

4. Donna Jackel. "Colon pleads guilty." *Rochester Democrat & Chronicle*, 14 August 1998.

Chapter 22

1. Stout, G./LaVallee, D. interview by S.C. Tarbell and L.L. Wallace. 7 December 2016.

2. Effman, N. interview by L.L. Wallace. 5 October 2016.

3. Todd Fielding. "Reactions to pleas range from shock to relief." *The Daily News*, 14 August1998.

4. Donna Jackel. "Colon pleads guilty." *Rochester Democrat and Chronicle*, 14 August1998.

5. Paul Mrozek. "Prosecutor praises community." *The Daily News*, 27 August 1998.

6. Various Wyoming County Court documents.

7. Frank, H. interview by S.C. Tarbell and L.L. Wallace. 23 January 2017.

Made in the USA
Middletown, DE
14 July 2017